Scalable Processing of Spatial-Keyword Queries

Synthesis Lectures on Data Management

Editor
H.V. Jagadish, *University of Michigan*

Founding Editor
M. Tamer Özsu, *University of Waterloo*

Synthesis Lectures on Data Management is edited by H.V. Jagadish of the University of Michigan. The series publishes 80–150 page publications on topics pertaining to data management. Topics include query languages, database system architectures, transaction management, data warehousing, XML and databases, data stream systems, wide scale data distribution, multimedia data management, data mining, and related subjects.

Scalable Processing of Spatial-Keyword Queries
Ahmed R. Mahmood and Walid G. Aref
2019

Data Exploration Using Example-Based Methods
Matteo Lissandrini, Davide Mottin, Themis Palpanas, and Yannis Velegrakis
2018

Data Profiling
Ziawasch Abedjan, Lukasz Golab, Felix Naumann, and Thorsten Papenbrock
2018

Querying Graphs
Angela Bonifati, George Fletcher, Hannes Voigt, and Nikolay Yakovets
2018

Query Processing over Incomplete Databases
Yunjun Gao and Xiaoye Miao
2018

Natural Language Data Management and Interfaces
Yunyao Li and Davood Rafiei
2018

Scalable Processing of Spatial-Keyword Queries

Ahmed R. Mahmood and Walid G. Aref

ISBN: 978-3-031-00739-2   paperback
ISBN: 978-3-031-01867-1   ebook
ISBN: 978-3-031-00094-2   hardcover

DOI 10.1007/978-3-031-01867-1

A Publication in the Springer series
SYNTHESIS LECTURES ON DATA MANAGEMENT

Lecture #56
Series Editor: H.V. Jagadish, *University of Michigan*
Founding Editor: M. Tamer Özsu, *University of Waterloo*
Series ISSN
Print 2153-5418   Electronic 2153-5426

Scalable Processing of Spatial-Keyword Queries

Ahmed R. Mahmood and Walid G. Aref
Purdue University

SYNTHESIS LECTURES ON DATA MANAGEMENT #56

ABSTRACT

Text data that is associated with location data has become ubiquitous. A tweet is an example of this type of data, where the text in a tweet is associated with the location where the tweet has been issued. We use the term spatial-keyword data to refer to this type of data. Spatial-keyword data is being generated at massive scale. Almost all online transactions have an associated spatial trace. The spatial trace is derived from GPS coordinates, IP addresses, or cell-phone-tower locations. Hundreds of millions or even billions of spatial-keyword objects are being generated daily. Spatial-keyword data has numerous applications that require efficient processing and management of massive amounts of spatial-keyword data.

This book starts by overviewing some important applications of spatial-keyword data, and demonstrates the scale at which spatial-keyword data is being generated. Then, it formalizes and classifies the various types of queries that execute over spatial-keyword data. Next, it discusses important and desirable properties of spatial-keyword query languages that are needed to express queries over spatial-keyword data. As will be illustrated, existing spatial-keyword query languages vary in the types of spatial-keyword queries that they can support.

There are many systems that process spatial-keyword queries. Systems differ from each other in various aspects, e.g., whether the system is batch-oriented or stream-based, and whether the system is centralized or distributed. Moreover, spatial-keyword systems vary in the types of queries that they support. Finally, systems vary in the types of indexing techniques that they adopt. This book provides an overview of the main spatial-keyword data-management systems (SKDMSs), and classifies them according to their features. Moreover, the book describes the main approaches adopted when indexing spatial-keyword data in the centralized and distributed settings. Several case studies of SKDMSs are presented along with the applications and query types that these SKDMSs are targeted for and the indexing techniques they utilize for processing their queries.

Optimizing the performance and the query processing of SKDMSs still has many research challenges and open problems. The book concludes with a discussion about several important and open research-problems in the domain of scalable spatial-keyword processing.

KEYWORDS

spatial-keyword, indexing, systems, big data, query processing

To my wife, my parents, and my children.

Ahmed R. Mahmood

To my beloved parents, professors Safaa Elhifni and Galal Aref, and my lovely grandchildren, Hana and Walid.

Walid G. Aref

Contents

Preface

Scalable processing of spatial-keyword data is an important problem that is being studied actively by database researchers and industrial practitioners. This book targets developers and researchers that are interested in the design of scalable spatial-keyword data management systems (SKDMSs). The book surveys and classifies the main spatial-keyword queries, query languages, indexing techniques, and processing models, and aims to aid developers and researchers improve the scalability, efficiency, and performance of SKDMSs. There are many open research problems in the area of spatial-keyword processing. In this book, we highlight some of these problems to motivate the engagement of database designers and researchers in addressing them. It does not require prior knowledge about spatial-keyword processing or systems. Basic knowledge of database systems and data indexing techniques are all that are needed.

Ahmed R. Mahmood and Walid G. Aref
January 2019

Acknowledgments

Walid G. Aref's research has been partially supported by the National Science Foundation under Grant III-1815796.

CHAPTER 1

Introduction

1.1 SPATIAL-KEYWORD DATA

GPS-enabled smart devices, e.g., smartphones and smart tablets, have become very popular. Users spend tremendous amounts of time reading, typing, and texting on these devices. GPS devices associate the geographic location of the user to the data being typed or texted. As a result, a new type of data has emerged and become very popular, namely spatial-keyword data. Moreover, a new trend, termed *mobile-first*, has evolved among most technological companies that gives high priority to the development of applications and services on smart devices that make heavy use of this spatial-keyword data.

Spatial-keyword data can be defined as data that associates a set of keywords or sentences to a spatial location. One example of spatial-keyword data is microblogs, e.g., tweets. A tweet has a set of keywords that is the textual content of the tweet. In addition, a tweet is often associated with a spatial component, which is the location of the user that issued the tweet. Other examples of spatial-keyword data include web searches and points of interest. In addition to the textual and the location components, several other types of data may be augmented to spatial-keyword data. Two common examples are: (1) the object identifier of the object that owns the spatial-keyword data or that has emitted it; and (2) the timestamp of when this spatial-keyword data has been produced.

More formally, a data object, say o, that is of a **spatial-keyword data type**, is of the form $o = [oid, loc, text]$, where oid is o's identifier, loc is o's geo-location, and $text$ is the set of keywords associated with o. A spatial-keyword data object may be associated with other attributes, e.g., the timestamp when o is created.

Spatial-keyword data can either be *static* or *dynamic*. Static spatial-keyword data does not change its spatial location or its textual content over time, e.g., points of interest (POIs). A POI may have a fixed location and a fixed textual description. In contrast, dynamic spatial-keyword data continuously add new objects, e.g., tweets, or update the location or the associated text of existing objects. For example, when tourists are looking for nearby POIs, the locations of the tourists change as they move. Also, the search keywords of the tourists can change over time, e.g., at times, they may be looking for *museums*, while at other times, they may be looking for *restaurants* or *hotels*.

Currently, spatial-keyword data is being generated at an unprecedented rate. Almost all online transactions are associated with a spatial trace that can be inferred from the associated GPS coordinates, cell tower locations, and IP addresses. Augmenting the location data transforms text-only transactions into spatial-keyword transactions. For example, web-searches constitute spatial-keyword data when associating the keywords of the web-search with the spatial information inferred from the IP address where the web search has been initiated. The same applies to other online transactions, e.g., online shopping and video streaming. The textual attribute comes from the description of the item being searched or the title of the video being streamed, and the spatial attribute comes from the spatial trace, e.g., IP address or GPS coordinates, of the online transaction. This association has significantly increased the amount of the spatial-keyword data being generated. Figure 1.1 illustrates the scale by which spatial-keyword data is being generated. The figure illustrates that hundreds of millions of tweets and billions of web searches are being generated daily. Also, Facebook has on average 1.4 billion daily active users. These users generate over 200 million daily messages [1, 58], most of which are spatial keywords.

Figure 1.1: The scale of spatial-keyword data being generated daily. Based on [7].

1.2   SPATIAL-KEYWORD APPLICATIONS

There is a broad range of applications that benefit from the massive amounts of spatial-keyword data being generated. In this section, we describe some of these spatial-keyword-driven applications. Although many of the applications have existing systems that support them, scaling and optimizing the performance of these systems remain an important issue. For example, many software companies pay cloud service-providers to rent computing infrastructure to host their applications. Thus, optimizing the processing of these applications would have a significant cost reduction for companies providing these spatial-keyword applications. In this section, we describe some popular spatial-keyword applications.

Location-aware Targeting of Advertisements
One of the main reasons we have free Internet services, e.g., web search and video streaming, is the presence of online advertisements. The profits of many software companies, e.g., Google and

Facebook, depend mainly on the revenues coming from online advertisements. Typically, advertisers launch campaigns that target users with specific interests. Sometimes, these campaigns are location-driven, i.e., they target potential customers in specific regions. For example, a shoe manufacturer may target users with advertisements about running shoes when the user happens to be located in a sports arena. Thus, when a user is located in this vicinity and has a textual profile that demonstrates potential interest in running shoes, the user would receive an advertisement from the campaign. This type of advertising is termed location-aware advertisement targeting. Typically, there would be millions of users and targeting campaigns. Usually, campaigns run for significantly long durations, where the advertisers are often interested in monitoring the status of their campaigns in real time. This puts high demand on the spatial-keyword data management system (SKDMS), especially the fact that the server has to handle simultaneously the incoming streams of users' updates in their spatial-keyword data profiles. Naturally, users' locations change over time as well as their textual-profiles. These updates need to be processed in real time by the SKDMS. In summary, targeting of advertisements requires high scalability. It also needs to adhere to business performance requirements, i.e., having a real-time response about the dissemination of advertisements and campaign monitoring.

Crowd-powered Navigation

Mobile navigation-services, e.g., Google Maps [12], Apple Maps [13], and Waze [11], have become very popular among users of smartphones. One class of mobile navigation applications, termed crowd-powered navigation applications, allows the crowd, e.g., the commuters, to share their locations, and to associate some textual descriptions about the events happening at these locations, e.g., accidents, traffic, and road conditions. Users of the same application can get notifications about the nearby events and road conditions. Figure 1.2 illustrates Waze [11], an example crowd-powered navigation application. Crowd-powered navigation applications require high scalability and real-time responsiveness to allow a large number of users to instantaneously receive notifications about road events.

Spatial Web Search

Geotagging an object or text is the process of assigning spatial coordinates to the object or the text. The association of a spatial trace to online transactions, e.g., web search and online video streaming, and the advancement in geotagging have led to the development of locality-aware search engines [193–195]. These search engines consider both the spatial and textual attributes of the objects to improve the locality and the relevance of the search results.

Also, POIs constitute a major source of spatial-keyword data. There are several applications that depend on POIs. One example application is the identification of nearby attractions. In this application, users are interested in finding nearby POIs, e.g., hotels, museums, or cafes. The relevance of a POI is calculated based on a function of (1) the distance between the location of the user and the location of the POI and (2) the textual similarity between the descrip-

Figure 1.2: Waze: an example application of a crowd-powered navigation system. Based on [11].

tion of the POI and the user's search keywords. Figure 1.3 illustrates the user interface for the AroundMe mobile application [15] that finds the nearby POIs. Trip planning [9] is another application that depends on POIs. One popular scenario of trip planning is for a user to search for groups of POIs that are close to each other and that collectively cover a set of search keywords, e.g., when visiting a city, one would be interested in finding a hotel, a restaurant, and a cafe that are very close to each other.

Figure 1.3: AroundMe: an example application for searching for nearby POIs. Based on [15].

Analysis of Microblogs
Microblogs, e.g., tweets, are becoming a major source of spatial-keyword data. Various types of spatial-keyword analyses are currently being performed over microblogs. One example applica-

tion is identifying the trending keywords for different regions. Figure 1.4 demonstrates the user interface of the TrendsMap application [5] that provides the most popular keywords tweeted in various areas of the United States. Notice that these keywords are not static and change over time based on the trending topics at a given time. Other applications that involve microblogs analysis include: (1) the detection of news from microblogs [75, 177, 178, 196, 199]; (2) disaster tracking and management [200, 201], where users post microblogs about any crisis or critical situation they are in, e.g., a flood or wildfire; (3) medical research, where the analysis of tweets can provide insights on the spread of diseases, e.g., flu; (4) using microblogs to detect the abbreviated names for points of interest [180]; and (5) the detection of influential users from microblogs [178, 179].

Figure 1.4: TrendsMap: an application for microblogs analysis. Based on [5].

Massively parallel Location-based Games

A location-based game requires the knowledge of the location of the player as a crucial input to the game. Massively parallel games involve a large number of players that play the game simultaneously. Figure 1.5 illustrates the interface of the massively parallel game Pokemon Go [6]. In this game, millions of users share their locations and commute to search for virtual creatures (Pokemons) on the map. A player may wish to commute to a nearby location that contains valuable virtual creatures. Creatures have a textual description describing their names, types, and powers. Creatures and players keep changing their locations over time. A massively parallel location-based game requires high scalability and realtime responsiveness when processing the massive amounts of dynamic spatial-keyword data in the game.

In Chapter 2, we describe how spatial-keyword queries formalize and address these spatial-keyword applications.

Figure 1.5: Pokemon Go: a massively parallel location-based game. Based on [6].

CHAPTER 2

Querying Spatial-Keyword Data

With the existence of large volumes of spatial-keyword data, several query types have emerged to empower many spatial-keyword applications. In this section, we present an overview of the important types of spatial-keyword queries. Typically, in data management systems, queries are expressed using declarative query languages, e.g., SQL [20]. A query is composed of multiple query predicates that are combined using conjunctives, disjunctives, for-all ($\forall$), and there-exists ($\exists$) constructs. For example, in relational databases, these query predicates are the select, join, project, and group-by predicates. Complex queries can be composed as combinations of these query predicates.

For spatial-keyword queries, although there is a wide range of spatial-keyword query types, there exist only a few query languages that are able to express complex spatial-keyword queries as compositions of simple spatial-keyword query predicates. In this chapter, we describe and classify the main spatial-keyword query predicates. Then, we present an overview of existing spatial-keyword query languages and their supported set of queries.

2.1 SPATIAL-KEYWORD QUERY PREDICATES

There exists a wide range of spatial-keyword query types [30, 35, 69]. In this section, we present the main spatial-keyword query types that we use throughout the rest of this book. To compose queries on spatial-keyword data, one can use combinations of spatial-keyword query-predicates. The three main spatial-keyword query predicates are (1) spatial-keyword select predicates, (2) spatial-keyword group predicates, and (3) spatial-keyword join predicates. Below, we explain each predicate type and give instances of spatial-keyword queries that belong to this type.

2.1.1 THE SPATIAL-KEYWORD SELECT PREDICATE

The spatial-keyword select predicate operates on one set of spatial-keyword data objects, say R. Each spatial-keyword data object, say o, in R has an associated spatial location, say o_l, and an associated set of keywords, say o_k. o qualifies the select predicate if o satisfies the predicate's spatial and textual conditions. For example, consider a spatial-keyword select predicate that specifies a spatial range, say a two-dimensional rectangle w, and a set of keywords, say K. o

qualifies this spatial-keyword select predicate when the spatial location of o, i.e., o_l is inside the rectangle w, and o_k contains all the query keywords K.

Another qualification criterion is to rank the spatial-keyword objects in Set R according to some ranking score. The objects with the highest scores qualify as results to the query. The score of a spatial-keyword object is calculated as a function of the spatial proximity and the textual similarity between the object and the query. However, the qualification of an object depends solely on the properties of this particular object, not on the collective properties of groups of objects as in the spatial-keyword group predicate that will be explained subsequently.

The spatial-keyword select predicates can be used in many of the applications described in Chapter 1, e.g., location-aware ad-targeting, the identification of nearby attractions, spatial web-search, and microblogs analysis. In this section, we give examples of several spatial-keyword select predicates.

The Spatial-Keyword Filter Predicate

The spatial-keyword filter predicate consists of both a spatial range and an associated set of keywords. For a spatial-keyword object to qualify as a result to this query, the object needs to be located inside the spatial range of the query. Also, the object needs to satisfy a textual matching criterion. For example, a query may require that the set of keywords in the qualifying object contains all the keywords specified in the query. In this scenario, the predicate is termed a **Boolean range predicate**. There are other varieties of textual-matching criteria, e.g., having some overlap between the keywords associated with the objects and the keywords specified in the query predicate, or that the keywords associated with the objects satisfy a certain boolean expression on the keywords of the predicate. The spatial-keyword filter predicate is useful in location-aware ad-targeting applications.

Figure 2.1 gives example queries that involve the spatial-keyword filter predicate. In this example, Queries $q1$, $q2$, and $q3$ search for objects that are located inside the spatial ranges of the queries. Additionally, Queries $q2$ and $q3$ search for objects having keywords containing all the query keywords. Query $q1$ searches for objects having keywords that satisfy a textual boolean expression. The Boolean expression is to either contain the keyword *tea* or to contain both the keywords *coffee and sale*. Object $o1$ qualifies Queries $q1$ and $q2$ because $o1$ is located in $q1$'s and $q2$'s spatial ranges, and satisfies their desired textual criteria. Although Object $o2$ is located inside the spatial range of Queries $q2$ and $q3$, $o2$ does not qualify as output because $o2$ does not satisfy $q2$ or $q3$'s textual criteria.

The Spatial-Keyword Similarity Select Predicate [47]

In the spatial-keyword similarity select predicate, it is required to retrieve the spatial-keyword objects that are both spatially and textually similar to the query. In this query, objects are assumed to have surrounding spatial ranges that represent their locations, e.g., the service area of a cafe,

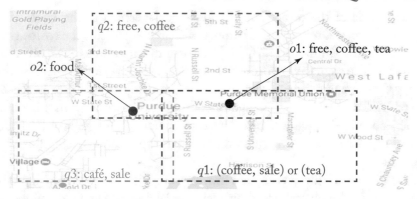

Figure 2.1: Example of a spatial-keyword filter predicate.

and the spatial similarity is defined by the degree of overlap between the spatial range of the query and the spatial ranges of the objects.

Figure 2.2 gives an example of the spatial-keyword similarity-select predicate. In this figure, only Object $o2$ qualifies as a result of Query $q1$ because $o2$ overlaps spatially and textually with Query $q1$. Notice that Object $o3$ does not have textual similarity with the keywords of Query $q1$. Also, Object $o1$ does not overlap spatially with the spatial range of Query $q1$.

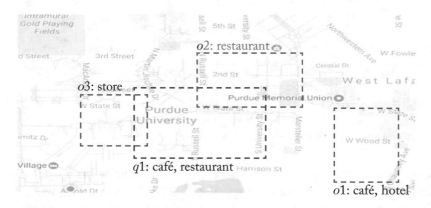

Figure 2.2: The spatial-keyword similarity predicate.

The Spatial-Keyword Top-k Select Predicate [33, 34, 49, 56, 102, 103, 124, 135, 143, 151, 182]
When answering queries that involve the spatial-keyword top-k predicate, spatial-keyword objects are ranked based on a function of their spatial and textual proximities to the query. The spatial proximity is often calculated based on the distance between the location of the object and a query-specific location. The textual proximity is calculated based on the textual similarity

between the keywords of the object and the keywords specified in the query. There are several textual similarity measures, e.g., the number of shared keywords, the cosine similarity [29], and the textual semantic similarity [128, 154] between the keywords of the object and the keywords of the query. The spatial-keyword top-k predicate searches for k objects with the highest ranking scores. One specific type of the spatial-keyword top-k predicate is the *Boolean kNN spatial-keyword predicate* [124]. In this predicate, ranking is based only on the spatial proximity between the objects and the query. Objects need to contain all the keywords of the query. The spatial-keyword top-k predicate can be used in touristic applications, e.g., in searching for the nearby attractions.

Figure 2.3 gives example queries that involve the spatial-keyword top-k predicate. In the figure, Query $q1$ ranks the objects based on their spatial distance and the number of keywords shared between the objects and the query. The top-three ranked objects are $o5$, $o2$, and $o1$. Object $o5$ is the top-ranked object because $o5$ contains all the query keywords, and is the object closest to the location of the query. Notice that, in this query, objects are ranked individually and not in groups.

Figure 2.3: The spatial-keyword top-k select predicate.

Direction-aware spatial-keyword search [142] is a variant of the spatial-keyword top-k select predicate that identifies objects in a specific direction. For example, when a user is on a highway and the user is looking for a "gas station," the user would be interested in the top-k relevant spatial-keyword objects that are located in the user's driving direction to minimize the detour time. The relevance of spatial-keyword objects is based on the spatial proximity and the textual similarity between the objects and the query. The social-aware spatial-keyword top-k select predicate [151] is another variant of the spatial-keyword top-k select predicate that accounts for the friendship relations among users of a social network. This query gives higher ranking to spatial-keyword objects that are generated from the query issuer's friends in the social network.

The Spatial-Keyword Reverse Top-k Select Predicate [144, 145]

The reverse top-k select predicate identifies the spatial-keyword objects that have the query point among their set of top-k relevant objects. This predicate has a spatial location and a set of keywords. To better understand this query, one can think that the query is added to the set of spatial-keyword objects, and for every spatial-keyword object, the set of top-k relevant spatial-keyword objects is identified. Only objects that have the query inside their top-k relevant-sets are returned as the query result. This query is motivated by the need to find the *influenced* set of objects that would be affected by the addition of a new spatial-keyword object. For example, this query can find the set of restaurants that would be affected by opening a new restaurant. Figure 2.4 gives example queries that involve the reverse top-k spatial-keyword predicate. In the figure, the top-three relevant objects for $o1$ are $q1$, $o2$, and $o3$. Also, the top-three relevant objects for $o4$ are $q1$, $o3$, and $o5$. Hence, the resultset of $q1$ contains the Objects $o1$ and $o4$ assuming that no other object has $q1$ in its top-three relevant list.

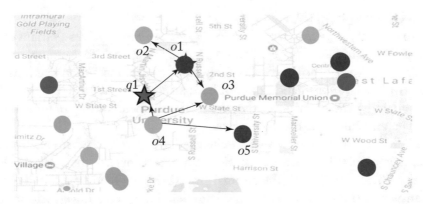

Figure 2.4: The reverse top-k spatial-keyword predicate.

2.1.2   THE SPATIAL-KEYWORD JOIN PREDICATES

In contrast to the spatial-keyword select predicate that has one set of spatial-keyword objects as input, the spatial-keyword join predicate [61, 71, 109, 121, 127, 152] accepts two sets of spatial-keywords objects as input, and produces pairs of spatial-keywords objects that satisfy a certain join predicate as output. The spatial-keyword join predicate can take a variety of forms. For instance, spatial-keyword objects can join if they are within a specific distance from each other and have some overlap between their keywords, e.g., share the same interests as expressed in their textual profiles. Another use of a binary spatial-keyword join predicate is that spatial-keyword objects join if an object from the first data source, is among the top-k relevant objects from the second data source [54]. One application of this variant of the spatial-keyword join predicate is providing real-time reviews about POIs. In this application, one data source is a tweets stream and the second data source is the POIs table. A tweet joins with a POI when the following conditions are satisfied: (1) there is an overlap between the keywords of the tweet and the keywords of the POI (e.g., if the tweets mentions the POI) and (2) the tweet is located in the vicinity of the POI.

2.1.3   THE SPATIAL-KEYWORD GROUP PREDICATE

The spatial-keyword group predicate does not consider properties of the individual objects. Instead, the spatial-keyword group predicate considers the collective properties of groups of objects. The result of a query that involves the spatial-keyword group predicate is one or more groups of spatial-keyword objects that satisfy a certain group membership criterion. The spatial-keyword group predicate is applicable in multiple scenarios, e.g., in trip planning, where users seek to identify groups of spatial-keyword objects that have specific collective spatial-keyword properties. In this section, we present several variants of the spatial-keyword group predicate.

The Clustered Group Query [132, 172, 174]

This query, also termed the *m-closest keywords (mCK) group query*, involves a variant of the spatial-keyword group predicate that searches for a single group of spatial-keyword objects. Objects in a group are closest to each other, and collectively cover a specific set of m keywords. The query consists of a set of m keywords, and does not have a specific location. Closeness of the group members is defined by the diameter of the group. The diameter of the group is the maximum distance between any pair of objects in the group.

Figure 2.5 gives an example of an m-clustered group query, where m is equal to 3. In this example, it is required to identify the closest group of objects that collectively cover the keywords "*cinema, restaurant, cafe.*" The optimal group is highlighted by a dotted circle. Finding the optimal answer to this query is an NP-hard problem [132]. Existing algorithms that answer this query give approximations to the optimal answer. The closeness of group objects can be defined using the diameter of the group, i.e., the maximum distance between any two objects in the group or the sum of distances between all pairs of objects in the group.

Choi et al. [118] address a variant of this query, termed the minimum spatial-keyword cover (SK-Cover). The objective of the SK-Cover query is to find a minimal group of spatial-keyword objects that are close to each other while covering all the query keywords. The main difference between SK-cover and mCK is that SK-covers aims to find fewer objects in the group than mCK. Objects covering more than one query keyword could be better candidates in the resultset of the SK-cover query. Finding the optimal answer to the SK-cover query is NP-Hard.

The Ranked-Group Query [101, 119, 122, 123, 165]

In this variant of the spatial-keyword group predicate, groups of spatial-keyword objects are required to collectively cover the set of query keywords. In contrast to the m-clustered spatial-keyword group predicate, this query predicate has a spatial location. To answer this query predicate, groups of objects are ranked. The ranking of the groups is based on a weighted function of

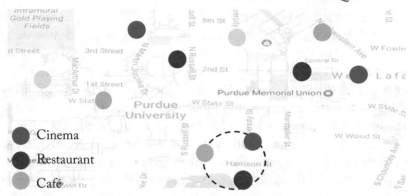

Figure 2.5: The m-clustered spatial-keyword group query.

(1) the distance, say d, between the group and the location of the query and (2) the closeness, say c, of members of the group to each other, e.g., as reflected by the diameter of the group. Figure 2.6 gives an example of the ranked-group query. In the figure, the location of the query is marked by a star, and the keywords of the query are "*cinema, restaurant, and cafe.*" Group $g1$ is closer to the location of the query. However, objects in Group $g1$ are not as close to each other as in Group $g2$. Group $g2$ is more suited if the user wishes to drive to the group, and then walk from one object in the group to the other.

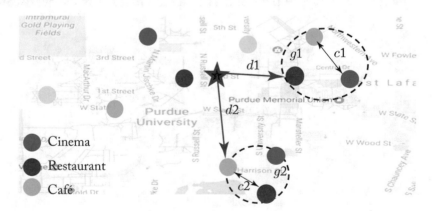

Figure 2.6: The single-ranked-group query.

Cao et al. [122, 123] address one version of the ranked-group query-predicate, also termed as the collective spatial-keyword group predicate (CoSKQ), that retrieves a single group with the highest score. Su et al. [120] address the collective spatial-keyword group predicate on road networks, also termed the group-based collective keyword query (GBCK, for short).

The level-aware collective spatial-keyword query (LCSK) [117] is another variant of the ranked-group query where the spatial-keyword objects being searched have weights, e.g., the number of stars of a hotel or the rating of a restaurant. In the level-aware spatial-keyword group predicate, it is required to retrieve a single group of objects that collectively cover the query keywords while optimizing a cost function. The cost function includes the following parameters: (1) the distance between the objects of the group and the location of the query and (2) the weights, i.e., the levels, of the spatial-keyword objects that constitute the group.

Skovsgaard et al. [165] address another version of the ranked-group query-predicate that searches for multiple groups of objects. These ranked groups are provided to the user to choose from. The optimal answer to the ranked-group query is NP-hard. Existing efficient solutions attempt to find approximate answers. Notice that in this query, ranks are over entire groups and not over individual objects.

The Spatial-Keyword Pattern-Matching Group Query [81]

This spatial-keyword group query searches for a group of spatial-keyword objects that satisfy a set of distance constraints, i.e., spatial patterns. Figure 2.7 gives an example of a spatial-keyword pattern-matching query, where a user is searching for an apartment with the following requirements: (1) the apartment is not located more than one mile from a park and (2) the apartment is no further than three miles away from a bus station and no closer than one mile away from a bus station. These requirements are represented as spatial patterns or spatial constraints that need to be satisfied when answering the query. The answer to this query is a group of spatial-keyword objects that contain an apartment, a park, and a bus station that satisfy the query constraints.

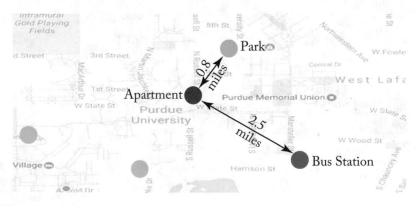

Figure 2.7: The spatial-keyword pattern matching group query.

2.1.4   CONTINUOUS SPATIAL-KEYWORD QUERIES

A spatial-keyword query can either be over a snapshot of time (and hence, the term snapshot query), or continuous over some time duration (and hence, the term continuous query). For example, a query that involves the spatial-keyword filter predicate can run as a snapshot query over static spatial-keyword data, e.g., over POIs. In contrast, a continuous spatial-keyword select [79, 99, 207, 208] or top-k [80, 169] query may operate over a stream of spatial-keyword data, e.g., tweets, and continuously produce results until the query gets revoked.

For continuous spatial-keyword queries, to deal with the infinite nature of the stream of upcoming spatial-keyword data, a window of focus for each query needs to be specified. The window of focus can be specified in a variety of ways. It can be either a time window [38, 40–42, 88–90], e.g., the tweets received in the last hour, or a tuple-count window [38, 39, 41, 91, 92, 96], e.g., the most recent 100 tweets. Alternatively, the window of interest can depend on a logical predicate, e.g., as in the case of predicate windows [45, 46, 93, 94], where the tuples of interest, e.g., spatial-keyword objects located inside a specific location, remain in the window of interest as long as the predicate is satisfied.

One application of time-sliding window maintenance over spatial-keyword data is building a diverse summary of spatial-keyword data, e.g., microblogs [89, 90]. This summary can be seen as a representative of the contents of the microblogs over the sliding window. Another application is identifying the trending topics in the microblogs [88].

The tuple-count window model has been adopted in top-k publish/subscribe applications [96], where superscriptions are represented by continuous spatial-keyword top-k queries. In this version of the spatial-keyword top-k query, it is required to identify the k-most relevant spatial-keyword publications, i.e., spatial-keyword objects among the most-recent N tuples, where N is the tuple-count window-size. The k-most representative and valuable streamed spatial-keyword documents [91] is a variation of the top-k spatial-keyword query that accounts for the reliability and importance of the relevant spatial-keyword objects. This query also operates over the tuple-count window model. The tuple-count window model has been adopted in the spatial-keyword selectivity estimation of the spatial-keyword filter query [92]. In this operation, histograms about the densities of the streamed spatial-keyword data is maintained over the tuple-count window.

Predicate windows over spatial-keyword data have been adopted in the tracking of moving spatial-keyword objects [93, 94] where the predicate is defined as a specific spatial range. Spatial-keyword objects remain in the window of focus as long as they satisfy the spatial predicate, i.e., the spatial-keyword objects are located inside the spatial range of the window predicate.

Another important parameter when answering continuous queries with windows is the manner by which the window slides over the continuous stream. For example, in the case of a tuple-count window of length 100 tuples, the window may slide by 100 tuples. In this case, it is a *tumbling* window, where once the window moves and because of the lack of overlap between the old and the new windows, the previous spatial-keyword query results are ignored and new ones are produced based on the new window only.

Alternatively, the window may slide by a value that is less than the size of the window. In this case, the new window partially overlaps with the old window. For example, suppose we are interested in the finding the most-frequent keywords in the last hour and the answer gets updated every five minutes. In this case, with every slide of the window, we need to subtract out from the output the keywords corresponding to the oldest five minutes that have expired, and add the new keywords corresponding to the most-recent five minutes.

2.1.5   AGGREGATE SPATIAL-KEYWORD PREDICATES

Aggregate operators are applicable to spatial-keyword query predicates. For example, the top-k frequent keywords operator is an aggregate spatial-keyword operator that identifies the most-frequent keywords over a specific spatio-temporal select predicate. This spatio-temporal select predicate can be specified based on the boundaries of a predefined grid partitioning of the space [146] or freely, i.e., at any point in the space [171]. This query is being adopted mainly in the analysis of microblogs, e.g., tweets, and can be used to identify the recent trending topics in the microblogs for specific spatial locations.

Zhang et al. [149] address the aggregate keyword nearest-neighbor predicate (AKNN). Given a set of spatial-keyword objects, a set of keywords, and a set of query locations, it is required to identify a single spatial-keyword object that covers all query keywords and has the minimum aggregate road-network distance to all query locations. For example, consider the road network in Figure 2.8. Assume that two individuals are looking to share an apartment that is "sunny," "quiet," and has a "kitchen." However, these two individuals are working at two different locations represented by the two query points $q1$ and $q2$. In Figure 2.8, both apartments $p1$ and $p5$ cover all query keywords. However, Apartment $p1$ is the query result as it covers all query keywords and has the least aggregate road-network distance to the query locations $q1$ and $q2$.

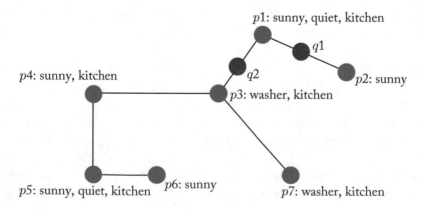

Figure 2.8: The spatial-keyword aggregate nearest-neighbor query.

2.1.6   DISTANCE METRICS IN SPATIAL-KEYWORD PREDICATES

The distance metric used when answering spatial-keyword queries is an important factor that can significantly affect the query-processing steps, i.e., varying the underlying distance-metric results in new variations of spatial-keyword queries. For example, the most widely adopted distance metric in spatial-keyword processing is the Euclidean distance (e.g., as in [74, 95, 97, 117, 119]). Another popular distance metric is the road-network distance (e.g., as in [65, 80, 120, 149, 163]). It is often the case that algorithms and indexes designed to answer spatial-keyword queries for a specific distance-metric are not applicable to another distance metric. For example, a multidimensional spatial index, e.g., the quadtree [48], is used to answer spatial-keyword queries when the query's distance metric is the Euclidean distance. However, multidimensional spatial indexes are useless when answering the same query, i.e., the spatial-keyword top-k query, over road networks [163], where the distance is measured by the shortest-path length on the network graph.

The same concept applies to textual similarity measures that are used in the spatial-keyword select and top-k predicates. Textual similarity measures vary with respect to the type of textual matching-criteria. Textual similarity measures include (1) exact keyword-match and (2) approximate keyword-similarity. In exact keyword-match, keywords of objects need to be identical to the query keywords. Textual similarity is based on the degree of overlap between the keywords of the query and the keywords of the object, e.g., the textual cosine-similarity [37]. Approximate keyword-similarity [62, 114, 173] accounts for typos that human users may make. The string edit-distance [170] is an approximate measure for textual similarity. It is based on the edit operations, e.g., the number of the inserts, deletes, and substitutions, needed to transform one string to another.

2.2   SPATIAL-KEYWORD QUERY LANGUAGES

One important aspect of data management systems is their ability to express the various types of queries using a query language. A query language for an SKDMS needs to accommodate for the hybrid nature of spatial-keyword queries. It integrates both the spatial and the textual attributes of the data being queried. Although there are many important spatial-keyword queries, there are few query languages that are able to express a wide range of spatial-keyword queries.

There exist multiple spatial-only and text-only query languages. Spatial-only query languages, e.g., [115, 130, 131, 155, 162], do not account for the textual aspect of the spatial-keyword queries, and hence cannot be used to express complex spatial-keyword queries. Many commercial and enterprise database systems contain extensions to support spatial queries, e.g., Oracle Spatial [175], SQL Server Spatial [113], MySQL Spatial [210], and PostGIS [209]. Spatial-only query languages provide two main components for expressing spatial queries: (1) abstract data types to represent spatial data, e.g., the point, rectangle, and polygon data types and (2) spatial predicates and functions, e.g., functions that calculate the distance between spatial objects. Similarly, text-only query languages, e.g., [155, 161, 168] do not consider the spatial attributes of spatial-keyword data, and cannot be used to express complex spatial-keyword queries. These text-only languages focus on retrieving objects or documents that are highly relevant to a specific set of keywords. For example, one text-only query is "Retrieve documents that contain the keyword *hotel*." Text-only queries can have Boolean expressions and approximate keyword-matching, e.g., having misspelled search-keywords. Many commercial and enterprise database systems provide full-text search abilities, e.g., Oracle [31] and SQL Server [32]. The existence of spatial-only and full-text search extension within a data management system does not allow the expression of complex spatial-keyword queries, e.g., the spatial-keyword group queries. To address this issue, several spatial-keyword query languages have been proposed to express complex spatial-keyword queries. In this section, we present an overview of three spatial-keyword query languages, namely, GNIP [4], MQL [150], and Atlas [68]. These languages differ in the types of queries they can support.

2.2.1 GNIP

GNIP [4] is a commercial filtering-tool for analyzing social-media posts and microblogs (mainly, tweets). GNIP supports realtime filtering of tweets using various flavors of the spatial-keyword filter query. GNIP offers powerful spatial-keyword filtering *rules* that include the spatial location, the textual content, and the language of the textual content. Users post their filtering rules to the **GNIP PowerTrack API [4]** in the JavaScript Object Notation format(JSON) [147]. Below, we give examples of the filtering predicates supported by GNIP.

- **Exact Keyword-filtering**: Identify all spatial-keyword objects whose textual attribute contain keywords "*hotel cafe*." This filtering rule is expressed as follows:

```
{
    "rules":
    [
        {"value":hotel cafe}
    ]
}
```

- **Substring Matching**: Identify the spatial-keyword objects whose textual attribute contains keywords that have "*day*" as a substring, e.g., as in "*birthday*." This filtering predicate is represented using the following predicate in GNIP: (*contains: day*). The syntax of this rule is as follows:

```
{
    "rules":
    [
        {"value":(contains: day)}
    ]
}
```

· **Approximate String-matching**: In GNIP, one can match keywords with typos. The following GNIP predicate: ("*happy birthday*"~ 3) allows finding spatial-keyword objects that have up to three different mismatching characters from the string "*happy birthday*." The approximate string matching rule is expressed as follows:

```
{
    "rules":
    [
        {"value":(happy~birthday ~ 3)}
    ]
}
```

· **Spatial Filtering**: Identify the spatial-keyword objects that are within Distance 5 from a certain location (x,y). This is represented using the following GNIP predicate:

```
{
    "rules":
    [
        {"value":(point_radius:[x, y, 5])}
    ]
}
```

· **Composition of Multiple Spatial and Textual Filters**. Spatial and textual predicates can be combined in GNIP to express more complex spatial-keyword filter queries. For example, consider the following predicate that composes spatial and textual predicates in GNIP:

```
{
    "rules":
    [
        {"value":((happy   OR    party)
        (holiday   OR  house   OR  new year's eve)
        point_radius:[105.27346517,   40.01924738,   10.0mi])}
        ]
}
```

This predicate identifies the spatial-keyword objects that have the following properties: (1) the objects are within 10 miles from Location (105.27346517, 40.01924738), (2) the objects contain one element of the following set of keywords {"happy," "party"}, and (3) the objects contain one element from the following set of keywords {"holiday," "house," "new year's eve"}.

In addition to the above filtering capabilities, GNIP provides more filtering tools that are specific to tweets, e.g., filtering by country, or by the language of the tweets. One limitation of GNIP is that it cannot represent some complex spatial-keyword queries, e.g., spatial-keyword group queries.

2.2.2   MICROBLOGS QUERY LANGUAGE (MQL)

Magdy et al. [150] introduce a specification of a system for the management of microblogs, e.g., tweets. This system includes memory-based and disk-based processing and indexing modules. Figure 2.9 illustrates the structure of the proposed microblogs management system. One of the main components of this system is a microblogs query language (MQL). MQL answers spatial-keyword queries that contain a specific temporal range over microblogs. These queries can either return the microblogs or aggregates over the microblogs. The syntax of MQL is as follows.

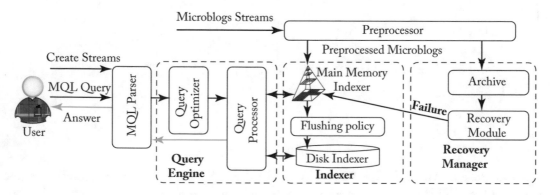

Figure 2.9: The structure of a microblogs management system [150].

```
SELECT [CONTINUOUS] attr_list
FROM source_name1 [,source_name2,...]
[WHERE condition]
ORDER BY F(arg_list)
LIMIT k
ON {LAST T {MINUTES | DAYS} | {T_start,T_end}}
```

SELECT [CONTINUOUS] `grouping_attr_list, AGGR_FUN(attr_list)`
FROM `source_name1 [,source_name2,...]`
[WHERE `condition]`
GROUP BY `grouping_attr_list`
LIMIT `k`
ON {LAST T {MINUTES | DAYS} | {T_start,T_end}}

MQL requires specifying a temporal range for all of its supported queries, e.g., the past hour. MQL supports both spatial and textual filtering predicates. The following statement gives an example query in MQL. In this query, it is required to continuously return the number of microblogs per keyword. This query is restricted by a specific spatial and temporal range. One limitation of MQL is that is cannot represent some complex spatial-keyword queries, e.g., spatial-keyword group queries.

```
SELECT CONTINUOUS keyword, COUNT(*)
FROM twitter_stream
WHERE location WITHIN (52,44.7,39.91,21.8)
ORDER BY keyword
LIMIT 10 ON ("18 Feb 2014",∞)
```

2.2.3 ATLAS

Mahmood et al. [68] introduce an extension to SQL that can express a wide range of complex spatial-keyword queries, e.g., spatial-keyword group queries, that are not expressible using other spatial-keyword query languages. The main idea behind Atlas is to provide simple building blocks that, when combined together, can express complex spatial-keyword queries. The syntax of Atlas is given below.

SELECT `{*|attr1 [AS alias][,attr2,...]}`
FROM `source_name1 [,source_name2,...]`
[WHERE `condition]`
[ORDER BY `F(arg_list)]`
[LIMIT `{k|condition}]`

```
SELECT grp_attr1 [AS alias][,grp_attr2,...],
AGGR_F [AS alias](attr_list)
FROM source_name1 [,source_name2,...]
[WHERE condition]
{PARTITION BY} grp_attr_list AS group_alias
[ORDER BY F(grp_arg_list)]
[LIMIT k]
[HAVING {condition}]
```

Atlas provides the following building blocks: (1) spatial and textual filtering predicates, (2) ordering via the ORDER BY construct to express the spatial-keyword top-k query, (3) the PARTITION BY, (4) WITHIN_DIST, and (5) the CONDITIONAL LIMIT operators, where Building Blocks (3)–(5) help express spatial-keyword grouping queries. Below, we present an overview of the spatial-keyword grouping constructs in Atlas.

The PARTITION BY SQL Operator

The PARTITION BY operator is similar to the traditional GROUP BY operator in standard SQL in that it identifies groups of objects. However, in contrast to the traditional GROUP BY operator that can only support aggregates over groups, the PARTITION BY operator returns the member objects of the groups. PARTITION BY is a standard SQL operator. However, Atlas makes use of this operator to construct and produce, as output, groups that satisfy certain properties that are qualified via the other building block operators in the Atlas query.

The WITHIN_DIST Operator

The WITHIN_DIST operator is used to identify groups of spatial-keyword objects, where the objects composing a group are within a specific distance from each other. This operator can be used to approximate the answer to spatial-keyword group queries that require searching for groups of spatial-keyword objects that are very close to each other [156]. A spatial-keyword group query can be expressed using the following Atlas statement [68].

```
SELECT * FROM POIs AS p
WHERE OVERLAP("food, cinema, hotel",p.text) >0
PARTITION BY WITHIN_DIST(Euclidean,p.loc,4) AS G
ORDER BY DIAMETER (Euclidean,G)
HAVING CONTAINS(UNION(G.text),"food, cinema, hotel")
LIMIT 3
```

This query identifies the three most spatially compact groups of spatial-keyword objects. First, the OVERLAP operator is used to identify objects whose textual attribute contains any of the query keywords. Then, the PARTITION BY and WITHIN_DIST operators are used to identify groups of objects. The maximum distance between any pair of objects in a group is four miles. The HAVING clause identifies candidate groups of objects that collectively cover the query keywords. Finally, the candidate groups are sorted based on their DIAMETER using the ORDER BY clause. Only the three most compact groups are returned as the query result using the LIMIT clause.

The CONDITIONAL LIMIT Operator

The CONDITIONAL LIMIT operator extends the standard LIMIT operator in SQL. The standard LIMIT operator returns tuples up to a specific number as in the following SQL statement that returns the three highest-paid employees.

```
SELECT * FROM Employee AS E
ORDER BY E.salary
LIMIT 3
```

The CONDITIONAL LIMIT uses a condition as a stopping criterion instead of a number, where the objects that qualify the query predicates are produced as output until these output objects collectively satisfy the stopping criteria of the CONDITIONAL LIMIT phrase. In spatial-keyword processing, one condition would be to check if all objects collectively contain all query keywords as in the following Atlas statement [68].

```
SELECT * FROM POIs AS p
WHERE OVERLAP("food, cinema, hotel",p.text)>0
ORDER BY DIST(Euclidean,q.loc,p.loc)
LIMIT CONTAINS(UNION(p.text,"food, cinema, hotel"))
```

This query identifies a set of spatial-keyword objects that collectively cover the keywords "food, cinema, hotel." The member objects of the group are the closest to the location of the query.

CHAPTER 3

Centralized Spatial-Keyword Query Processing

Centralized systems have been developed to process queries over spatial-keyword data. A centralized system runs on a single computing machine, and the processing is restricted by the resources of this machine. To address scalability in query processing, spatio-temporal indexing techniques have been developed along with the spatial-keyword query processing algorithms that operate over these indexes, e.g., as in [125, 198].

In the data management literature, there exists numerous types of indexes that are often optimized for specific use-cases or specific operations. For example, the hash table [16, 17] and the B-tree [98, 148] (and its variants) are used in relational database management systems. The hash table is more suited for direct lookup operations, i.e., searching for individual data tuples. The B-tree is well suited for range searching of tuples that fall within a range of values based on a specific attribute. The R-tree [133], the quadtree [48], and the spatial grid are popular in spatial applications. Inverted lists [43] are popular in text-retrieval applications.

A spatial-keyword index often integrates a spatial index and a textual index to account for both the spatial and textual attributes of the indexed spatial-keyword objects. In this chapter, we present an overview of spatial-only and textual-only indexes as the building blocks for spatial-keyword indexing. Then, we classify and describe the main spatial-keyword indexes that are used in centralized systems. Finally, we conclude this chapter by presenting case studies of centralized SKDMSs.

3.1 SPATIAL INDEXING

Multi-dimensional data structures have long been used to index geospatial data, i.e., data that have longitude and latitude. Some spatial indexes are optimized for disk-based processing, e.g., the R-tree and its variants [116, 133]. Other types of spatial indexes are better suited for main-memory processing, e.g., the spatial-pyramid [141] and the quadtree [48]. The main difference between memory-based and disk-based indexes is the size of the index nodes. The size of nodes in disk-based indexes is usually equal to the size of one disk page. This aims at improving the process of reading index nodes from disk. However, nodes in main-memory indexes often have smaller sizes.

Spatial indexes can be categorized into *space-driven* and *data-driven* indexes. In space-driven indexes, boundaries of the index nodes do not depend on the distribution of data in space. Typically, in space-driven indexes, the indexed space is partitioned into non-overlapping regions. This may result in poor search performance in case the data is skewed. In order to partition the underlying space, space-driven indexes require the prior knowledge of the size of the indexed space. Any object that is located outside of the indexed space cannot be added to the index without expensive treatment to expand the index's underlying space to accommodate this newly inserted object. The main advantage of space-driven indexes is the fast indexing time. Data-driven indexes do not assume prior knowledge of the indexed space, and can handle new data items at any given location. Boundaries of data-driven spatial indexes arrange themselves according to the indexed data. This results in more expensive indexing time for data-driven indexes. In this section, we present several popular spatial indexes.

3.1.1   SPACE-DRIVEN INDEXES

In space-driven indexes, the indexed space is partitioned into non-overlapping rectangles. Space-driven indexes require prior knowledge of the entire indexed space. In space-driven indexes, the partitioning of the space that defines boundaries of the index nodes is independent of the data distribution. Examples of space-driven indexes are presented below.

The Uniform-Grid Spatial-Index

The uniform-grid spatial-index [16] is one of the most basic spatial indexes. In this index, space is partitioned into equal-sized cells. Spatial data objects are mapped into the relevant grid cells. Inserting new objects into the spatial grid is straightforward when objects are of type Point. A point object is inserted into only one grid cell that spatially contains the point. However, for non-zero-sized spatial data objects, e.g., ones of type Rectangle, an object needs to be inserted into all grid cells that overlap the spatial range of the object. This requires high memory overhead. The granularity of the spatial grid, i.e., the number of grid cells per dimension, is a very important parameter. A coarse grid granularity results in lower memory-requirements with relatively poor search performance. The reason is that many objects would be indexed into the same grid cell. A finer grid granularity may have better search performance for queries that have small spatial ranges. However, the finer the granularity, the higher the memory requirements of the index. Notice that the spatial grid can be used for disk-based indexing, where the spatial grid becomes a *directory* for disk pages, and every grid cell points to one or more disk pages. Initially, all spatial objects corresponding to a grid cell are stored in a single disk page. However, when the number of spatial objects indexed within a specific grid cell exceeds the capacity of one disk page, an overflow disk page is created and is linked to the grid cell. The spatial grid index behaves poorly for skewed spatial data distributions. The worst-case scenario is when all points get indexed in a single grid cell. In this case, querying the spatial grid would requires a linear scan over all the spatial objects. Figure 3.1 gives an example of a spatial grid index. In the figure, the indexed spatial data objects are two-dimensional points, where each point is mapped into a single grid cell. The spatial grid index has been adopted in multiple spatial-keyword indexes, e.g., [52, 82].

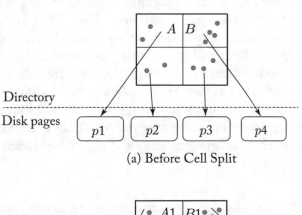

Figure 3.1: The spatial-grid index.

The Grid-File Index

The grid-file index [21] is a disk-based spatial index that improves over the disk-based version of the uniform grid spatial index [16]. The grid-file has been developed to better handle the skew in spatial data by allowing the spatial grid cells to split. Figure 3.2 illustrates the structure of the grid-file index. Similar to the disk-based uniform-grid spatial-index, the grid-file contains a directory that points to disk-pages. However, the main difference between the uniform-grid

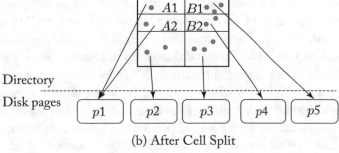

(a) Before Cell Split

(b) After Cell Split

Figure 3.2: The grid-file index.

spatial-index and the grid-file is how page overflows are handled. In the uniform-grid spatial-index, overflow pages are created and are linked to the same grid cell. In the grid-file, when a disk page overflows, the directory gets updated and split, and the overflowing cell is split in one dimension. For example, assume that the maximum disk-page-capacity is four in the grid-file of Figure 3.2. Figure 3.2a illustrates the directory and the disk pages of the grid-file before adding one spatial data object to Cell B. Inserting this spatial data object exceeds the capacity of Page $p4$. This results in splitting Cells A and B. Figure 3.2b illustrates the directory and the disk pages of the grid-file after splitting Cells A and B. Notice that Cells $A1$ and $A2$ point to the same disk page, i.e., Page $p1$. The reason is that Cell A does not exceed the disk page capacity. Cell B is split into two cells, i.e., $B1$ and $B2$. These cells point to two different disk pages, i.e., $p4$ and $p5$, respectively. The main limitation of the grid-file index is that the size of the directory can increase significantly due to splits while having many directory entries point to the same disk pages.

The Quadtree Index

The quadtree index [18, 22, 48] and its variants, e.g., [23, 197, 202–206] are hierarchical space-driven indexing structures. Leaf nodes in the quadtree contain the indexed spatial data objects. Non-leaf nodes in the quadtree are split into four equal-sized quadrants, namely: North-West (NW), North-East (NE), South-West (SW), and South-East (SW). Initially, a single node covers the entire space. This node receives all the incoming data. When the number of objects in a quadtree node exceeds a specific threshold, the node is split into four child nodes. In this case, all the indexed data objects in the parent node are redistributed into the corresponding child nodes. Figure 3.3 gives an example of a quadtree. Node A is the root of the quadtree and is split into four child quadrants. The quadtree index performs poorly when all the data is clustered in a very small area. This clustering results in having a very tall yet skinny quadtree with many empty nodes. The quadtree index has been adopted in many spatial-keyword indexes, e.g., [99, 107].

The Spatial Pyramid

The spatial pyramid [140] is a multi-level grid index, where one cell at any given level corresponds to four cells at the subsequent level. There are two variants of the spatial pyramid: (1) the leaf-only [140] pyramid and (2) the all-level pyramid [67, 79, 141, 146]. In the leaf-only pyramid, spatial data is indexed only at the leaf level of the pyramid. In the all-level pyramid, spatial data can be indexed at any level of the spatial pyramid. When building the spatial pyramid, the size of the indexed space and the height of the pyramid are assumed to be known a priori. A cell in the spatial-pyramid can be in one of the following states: (1) has children and (2) has data. Figure 3.4 illustrates the structure of the spatial pyramid. White spaces neither have any children nor have any data. Black cells contain data. Data cells do not have any children. Green cells are non-leaf nodes that have children but have no data. The spatial pyramid has been adopted in many spatial-keyword indexes, e.g., [79, 88, 146].

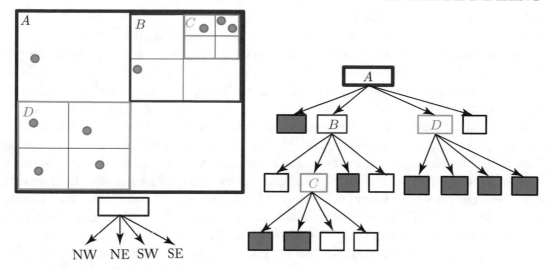

Figure 3.3: The quadtree index.

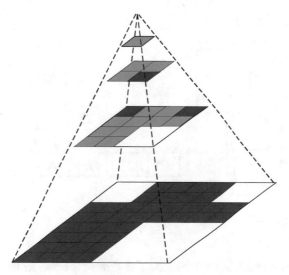

Figure 3.4: The spatial pyramid.

3.1.2 DATA-DRIVEN SPATIAL INDEXES

In data-driven spatial indexes, boundaries of the index nodes depend on the distribution of objects in the space. In this section, we give examples of several data-driven spatial indexes.

The R-Tree Index and its Variants

The R-tree index [116, 133] is one of the most widely adopted spatial indexes in relational database systems. The R-tree is a disk-based hierarchical index that is similar to the B-tree [98] index. Nodes of the R-tree are often equal to the size of one disk page. Each R-tree node has a minimum bounding-rectangle (an MBR, for short) that tightly surrounds all the spatial data inside the node. Initially, spatial data is inserted into one node, termed the root node. When the number of elements inside an R-tree node exceeds its capacity, the node is split into multiple child nodes. An important aspect that differentiates variants of the R-tree from one another is how the node splits upon an overflow. The main objective of the node splitting algorithms is to minimize the overlap among the MBRs of the resulting children nodes. The lower the overlap between the boundaries of the node, the less the number of nodes to be visited during a search operation. This leads to better search performance. One main limitation of the R-tree index is that the node-splitting algorithms for finding boundaries of children nodes are expensive because these algorithms need to minimize the overlap among the child nodes. The node-splitting algorithm increases the time needed to perform the insert operation. This aspect makes the R-tree inefficient in streaming scenarios, e.g., when many objects get inserted and deleted. Figure 3.5 illustrates the structure of the R-tree.

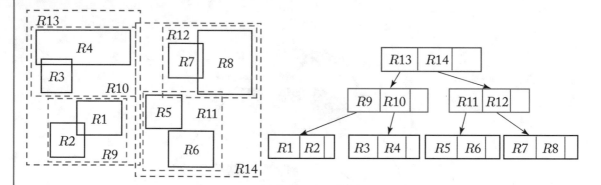

Figure 3.5: The R-tree index.

The original R-tree index is disk-based. The size of a node in the R-tree equals the size of one disk page. The cache-conscious R-tree (CR-tree) [84] is a variation of the R-tree that is optimized for main-memory indexing. The main idea behind the CR-tree is to shorten the height of the tree to reduce the number of cache misses. The CR-tree increases the fanout of the tree nodes by using a compressed representation of MBRs. This compression improves the overall performance of the CR-tree, and reduces its memory footprint. The R-tree index has been adopted in many spatial-keyword indexes, e.g., [50, 74, 126, 129, 143].

The kd-Tree Index

The kd-tree [157, 158] is a binary tree used for indexing multidimensional data, and is often used in spatial applications. The kd-tree assumes prior knowledge of the entire indexed space. When a node, say P, becomes full in the kd-tree, P is split into two children nodes based on only one spatial dimension at a time. The split dimension may change with each split. The kd-tree is a data-driven spatial index, where nodes are not split into spatially equal parts. However, the node-splitting algorithm of the kd-tree attempts to have an equal number of objects in each child node. The dimension for node splitting changes from level to level. For example, in the case of a two-dimensional kd-tree, nodes are split horizontally in one level, and in the subsequent level nodes are split vertically. Figure 3.6 illustrates the structure of the kd-tree. In this figure, we demonstrate one possible partitioning of the space and its corresponding kd-tree. Notice that the color of splits of the space resembles the parent-child relationship in the kd-tree nodes and the direction of node splitting, i.e., whether it is a horizontal or a vertical split. The kd-tree has been used in multiple spatial-keyword indexes, e.g., [53, 59, 71, 110].

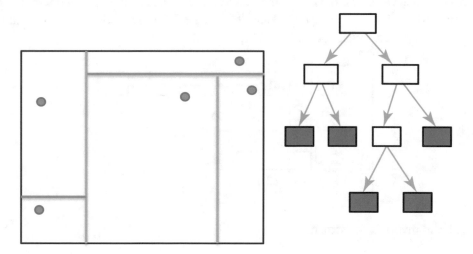

Figure 3.6: The kd-tree index.

3.2   TEXT INDEXES

Text indexes constitute an important component in spatial-keyword indexes. The main objective of text indexes is to support the efficient retrieval of textual objects based on whether or not the objects contain a specific set of keywords. In this section, we present the main text indexes used in spatial-keyword processing.

The Inverted List

The inverted list [43, 167] is one of the most widely adopted text indexes. Typically, the inverted list is structured as a hashmap of keywords. Every keyword has an associated list of objects that contain this keyword. The list of objects per keywords is often termed the *posting list* of the keyword. In the inverted list, every object is added to all of its keywords' posting lists. The inverted list is mainly designed to facilitate the *subset containment search operation* [83]. The subset containment search retrieves a subset of the indexed objects that contain all the query keywords. Refer to Figure 3.7 for illustration. In the figure, Object $o2$ is attached to the posting lists for Keywords $k1$ and $k2$. To find objects containing a single keyword, the posting list for this keyword is returned. To find objects containing more than one keyword, e.g., $k1$ and $k2$, the posting lists for Keywords $k1$ and $k2$ are intersected. In this example, only Object $o2$ contains both $k1$ and $k2$. Complex Boolean expressions can be evaluated using the union and the intersection of posting lists. For example, to find objects satisfying the expression ($k1$ and $k2$) or $k4$, i.e., the objects containing both the keywords $k1$ and $k2$ or alternatively containing the keyword $k4$. The posting lists for Keywords $k1$ and $k2$ are intersected. Then, the result is unioned with the posting list for Keyword $k4$. The resulting objects are $o2$ and $o3$. The inverted list has been adopted in several spatial-keyword indexes, e.g., [82, 111, 134, 136, 143].

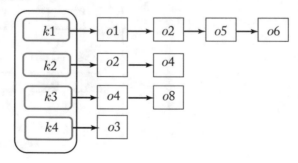

Figure 3.7: The inverted list structure.

The Ranked-Key Inverted-List

In the textual search domain, there are two main textual search problems: superset containment search and subset containment search. In the subset containment queries, a set of indexed objects containing all query keywords are retrieved. In contrast, in the superset containment search, it is required to retrieve a set of indexed objects whose keywords are fully contained in the query keywords. The ranked-key inverted list [85] is mainly designed to facilitate the *superset containment search problem* [83]. The ranked-key inverted list is a modification of the inverted list structure [112]. In contrast to the traditional inverted list, the ranked-key inverted list attaches objects to only a single keyword. In Figure 3.8, every object is attached to the posting list of a single keyword. One question arises: out of all the keywords of an object, which keyword does an object get attached to? To find out, all keywords are ranked by their overall frequencies of appearance, i.e., how many times every keyword appears in the entire indexed set of objects. Then, the object attaches to the posting list corresponding to the least frequent keyword that exists in the object. The ranked-key inverted list helps identify objects whose keywords are fully contained in the search keywords.

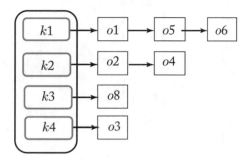

Figure 3.8: The ranked-key inverted list structure.

Refer to Figure 3.8 for illustration. Assume that the keywords in Object $o3$ are $k3$ and $k4$, and those in Object $o8$ are $k3$ and $k1$. In the figure, $o3$ and $o8$ are attached to the posting lists of Keywords $k4$ and $k3$, respectively. To retrieve the objects whose keywords are fully contained in $k3$ and $k4$, the posting lists for these keywords are retrieved. Then, all objects in the retrieved posting lists are checked to validate that the keywords in the objects are fully contained in the search keywords. In this case, $o3$ and $o8$ will be retrieved from the posting list of $k4$ and $k3$, respectively. However, only $o3$ qualifies as the result set of the query because $o8$ contains the Keyword $k1$ that is not in the search keywords. The ranked-key inverted list has lower memory requirements than the traditional inverted list [85].

The Inverted Bitmap
The inverted bitmap [86, 166] has a bit for every keyword in the indexed vocabulary. This means that the inverted bitmap index assumes prior knowledge of the entire vocabulary. For every keyword in an indexed object, bits corresponding to the keywords of the object are set to one. Figure 3.9 illustrates the structure of the inverted bitmap index. The inverted bitmap index has been used in some spatial-keyword indexes, e.g., the bR*-tree [174].

Text Signatures
A text signature [159] uses a bit vector to mark the existence of the keywords of indexed objects. Text signatures have a structure that is similar to the inverted bitmaps, described above. However, a text signature require less space than an inverted bitmap. To create a signature of a textual object, each keyword of the textual object is mapped to multiple locations in the bit vector using multiple mapping functions, e.g., hash functions. Then, these locations in the bit vector are set

$o1$ ($k1, k3, kn$)

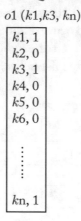

Figure 3.9: The inverted bitmap.

to 1. To check if a specific keyword exits in the set of the keywords of indexed objects, the mapping functions are used to identify relevant bit locations in the bit vector. A keyword is considered not found if any of the relevant bit locations in the bit vector is set to 0. Notice that having all the relevant locations of a keyword set to 1 does not guarantee the existence of the keyword. Text signatures differ from inverted bitmaps in the following aspects.

- The size of the bit vector in a text signature is much smaller than that of an inverted bitmap.

- A text signatures is an approximate, i.e., probabilistic, structure that may result in false positives. However, an inverted bitmap is an exact structure that does not result in false positives.

Text signatures have been used in some spatial-keyword indexes, e.g., the IR^2-tree [129].

The Ordered Keyword Trie
The trie [160] is a data structure that indexes strings based on their constituent characters. The ordered keyword trie [16] indexes textual objects based on their keywords. One can think of the ordered keyword trie as a traditional trie where the characters in the trie are replaced by keywords. The ordered keyword trie assumes a total order on the vocabulary of the keywords of the indexed objects. Figure 3.10 illustrates the structure of the ordered keyword trie. In this figure, Object $o2$ contains the keywords $k1$ and $k5$. The ordered keyword trie has high memory-requirement and good text-search performance [85]. Variants of the ordered keyword trie have been used in multiple spatial-keyword indexes, e.g., FAST [79] and the AP-tree [99].

3.3   SPATIAL-KEYWORD INDEXES

In general, the target of spatial-keyword data indexes is to efficiently process spatial-keyword queries over spatial-keyword data objects. Streams of both the spatial-keywords data objects and

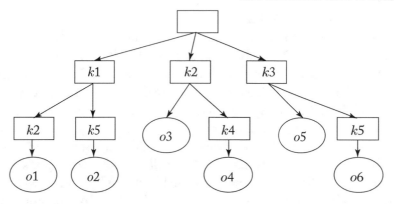

Figure 3.10: The ordered keyword trie.

the spatial-keyword queries arrive progressively and need to be processed efficiently. Usually, the queries are continuous in nature, i.e., once they get registered into the spatial-keyword query processing system, the queries continuously produce results as new qualifying spatial-keyword data objects arrive into the system.

There are two main approaches for indexing in spatial-keyword systems: (1) indexing the spatial-keyword data objects or (2) indexing the continuous queries. In the first approach, the spatial-keyword index indexes the spatial-keyword data objects, e.g., the points of interest, to improve the performance of the spatial-keyword queries. In contrast, in the second approach, the spatial-keyword index indexes the continuous queries. When new spatial-keyword data objects arrive, the query index is searched to determine which query and object pairs match each other. In this case, the matching pairs are reported as output.

Spatial-keyword indexes integrate a spatial index with a textual index. Widely adopted spatial indexes are the R-tree, the quadtree, and the spatial pyramid. These spatial indexes are integrated with a textual index, e.g., the inverted list, the ranked-key inverted list, the inverted bitmap, and the ordered keyword trie. Centralized spatial-keyword indexes can be classified into (1) space-first spatial-keyword indexes, (2) text-first spatial-keyword indexes, and (3) interleaved spatial-keyword indexes. In this section, we describe the main categories of spatial-keyword indexes, and give example spatial-keyword structures that represent each category.

3.3.1 SPACE-FIRST SPATIAL-KEYWORD INDEXING

Space-first spatial-keyword indexes give precedence to spatial indexing over textual indexing. In space-first spatial-keyword indexes, spatial indexing algorithms are first used. Then, text indexes are used inside some of the spatial index nodes to improve textual discrimination power of the overall spatial-keyword index. Space-first spatial-keyword indexes have better performance for queries that require higher spatial discrimination, e.g., spatial-keyword queries that do not cover a wide spatial range [125]. Below, we present examples of space-first spatial-keyword indexes.

The Spatial Pyramid with Inverted Bitmaps

The earliest spatial-keyword data structures has been reported by Aref and Samet [141]. In [141], the pyramid data structure [140] as the spatial index has been combined with an inverted bitmap [86] as the text index. An inverted bitmap has been associated with each quadrant of the pyramid. Bits in the bitmap of a quadrant are set to designate which of the keywords appear in this quadrant. A bitmap of one of the quadrants, say q, at a lower resolution is the union of the four bitmaps of the corresponding four child quadrants of q. The target applications of the spatial-keyword index in [141] have been a little different from today's location services and microblog-driven applications. It has been originally designed to help answer feature-based queries, e.g., queries of the form: Where are "corn fields" located? In this case, the bitmap corresponding to the root of the spatial pyramid is searched. If the bit corresponding to the keyword "corn fields" is set, then the pyramid is descended, and each of the bitmaps of the child nodes are checked for the same. Each child node is descended only when the bit corresponding to the keyword "corn fields" in this node's bitmap is set.

ST: Spatial Grid with Inverted Lists

In ST [82], spatial-keyword data objects are first distributed over a spatial grid. Then, all objects belonging to a specific cell of the grid are indexed using an inverted list. Figure 3.11 illustrates the structure of ST. ST has been designed mainly to answer the spatial-keyword filter query. This query is processed by first identifying the relevant spatial grid-cells that overlap the spatial range of the query. Then, the inverted lists of the overlapping cells are used to perform textual filtering. ST performs poorly when the spatial range of the query is large, i.e., the query does not have high spatial discrimination. The reason is that many inverted lists will need to be accessed. Also, if the indexed objects have spatial ranges instead of point locations, i.e., an object spans many grid cells, then the memory requirements of ST becomes significantly high due to the replication of objects across multiple spatial grid-cells.

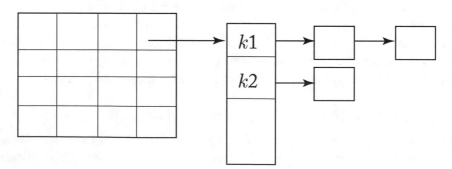

Figure 3.11: ST – Spatial grid with inverted lists [82].

The IR-Tree: An R-Tree with Inverted Lists

The IR-tree [143] is a spatial-keyword index that integrates the R-tree index with inverted lists. Figure 3.12 illustrates the structure of the IR-tree. In the IR-tree, spatial-keyword objects are spatially indexed using an R-tree. Then, the objects are textually indexed using an inverted-list structure. Within every node in the IR-tree, an inverted list is maintained to keep track of the keywords contained within the children nodes. These internal inverted-lists do not maintain direct references to the indexed spatial-keyword objects. However, the inverted list within an IR-tree node, say N, maintains for every keyword, say k, a list of all child nodes that contain the Keyword k. For example, in Figure 3.12, the root node contains an inverted list of the keywords of its children nodes, i.e., $R1$ and $R2$. The IR-tree has been used to answer multiple spatial-keyword queries including the spatial-keyword filter, the top-k, and groups queries.

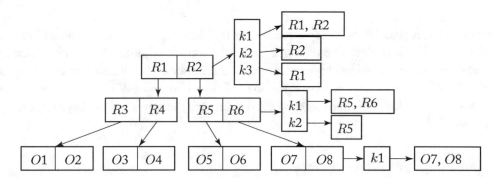

Figure 3.12: The IR-tree: R-trees with inverted lists [143].

The bR*-Tree: An R*-Tree with Text Bitmaps and Keyword MBRs

The bR*-tree [174] is a hybrid spatial-keyword index that integrates an R*-tree index [116] with inverted bitmaps. Figure 3.13 illustrates the structure of the bR*-tree. Spatial-keyword data objects are indexed using a traditional R*-tree with its regular insertion algorithm. Every node in the bR*-tree maintains a bitmap for every minimum bounding-rectangle (MBR) that corresponds to children nodes. The bitmap of a child MBR keeps track of all the keywords contained in the spatial-keyword data objects indexed under this child's MBR. For example, the child node pointed at by $R1$ contains only the keywords $k1$ and $k2$. To improve the pruning power of the bR*-tree, every keyword, say k, within a tree node has an associated MBR that surrounds all objects containing k. The bR*-tree has been used to answer the clustered spatial-keyword group queries, e.g., the m-closest keywords group query (see Section 2.1.3).

The IR^2-Tree: An R*-Tree with Text Signatures

The IR^2-tree [129] is a hybrid spatial-keyword index that integrates an R*-tree index [116] with text signatures [159]. Spatial-keyword data objects are indexed using a traditional R*-tree with

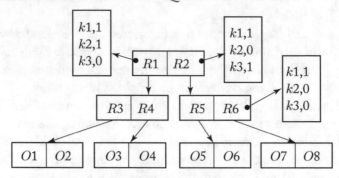

Figure 3.13: The bR*-tree: R-trees with bitmaps [174].

its regular insertion algorithm. Every node in the IR^2-tree represents an MBR and maintains a text signature. The text signature of a tree node keeps track of all the keywords contained in the spatial-keyword data objects indexed under the tree node. To calculate the text signature of a node, say N, in the IR^2-tree, the signatures of the children of N are combined using the logical OR operator. The IR^2-tree has been used to answer the top-k spatial-keyword query (see Section 2.1.1).

3.3.2 TEXT-FIRST INDEXING

Text-first indexes integrate a text index, e.g., the inverted list, with a spatial index, e.g., the spatial grid or the R-tree. Text-first indexes give higher priority to textual discrimination over spatial partitioning. Queries that require higher spatial discrimination, e.g., queries with small spatial range, perform poorly in this type of indexing [125]. In this section, we present examples of text-first spatial-keyword indexes.

TS: An Inverted List with Multiple Grid-Based Spatial Indexes
In the TS index [82], spatial-keyword data objects are first indexed by their textual data components using an inverted list. Then, all the spatial-keyword data objects attached to a specific keyword are indexed locally using a separate spatial grid. Figure 3.14 illustrates the structure of TS. TS is designed to answer the spatial-keyword filter query. A spatial-keyword filter query is processed by first identifying all the relevant keywords in the inverted list. Then, the spatial predicate is applied to all spatial grids that are associated with the relevant keywords. This indexing approach gives higher priority for highly-selective textual-predicates, e.g., when querying few or infrequent keywords. In this case, few spatial grids and spatial grid cells need to be checked and verified.

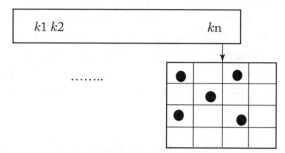

Figure 3.14: TS – Inverted list with grid-based spatial indexing [82].

S2I: An Inverted List with an R-Tree Index

S2I [74] is a text-first spatial-keyword index that integrates an inverted list with an R-tree. Figure 3.15 illustrates the structure of S2I. S2I accounts for the fact that the frequencies of the keywords are not uniform, and often follow a Zipfian distribution [79]. The Zipfian distribution has many infrequent keywords and only a few frequent keywords. In S2I, objects associated with frequent keywords are indexed using an R-tree. For every frequent keyword, a separate R-tree indexes the objects that contain this keyword. However, objects associated with infrequent keywords are grouped into disk-blocks. This index is mainly designed to address the spatial-keyword top-k query. To answer this query, objects are assigned scores. The score of an object increases based on how many query keywords are contained in the object and how close the objects are to the location of the query.

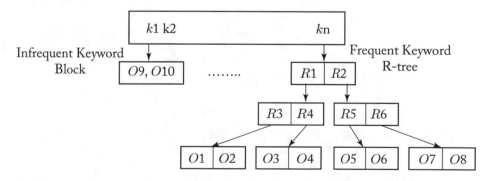

Figure 3.15: S2I: an inverted list with multiple R-tree indexes [74].

3.3.3 INTERLEAVED SPATIAL-KEYWORD INDEXING

Adopting a space-first or a text-first spatial-keyword index give higher priority to one aspect of the spatial-keyword data over the other aspect. Space-first spatial-keyword indexes do not perform well with queries that require high textual discrimination, e.g., queries that refer to infrequent keywords. Similarly, text-first spatial-keyword indexes do not perform well with queries that require higher spatial discrimination, e.g., queries having small spatial ranges. In this section, we present a class of spatial-keyword indexes that is neither space-first nor text-first. *Interleaved* spatial-keyword indexes arbitrate between spatial and textual partitioning according to the distribution of the spatial-keyword data objects in the spatial and textual dimensions.

The AP-Tree

The AP-tree [99] is an interleaved spatial-keyword index that addresses the limitations of space-first indexes and text-first spatial-keyword indexes by arbitrating between spatial and textual partitioning according to a cost function. The cost function attempts to maximize the discrimination between the indexed spatial-keyword data objects. The AP-tree integrates a quadtree with the ordered keyword trie. The AP-tree is designed to answer the continuous version of the spatial-keyword filter query. The structure of the AP-tree is illustrated in Figure 3.16. From the figure, observe that the tree nodes of the AP-tree are not of the same type or structure. A node in the AP-tree can either be a space-partitioning node or a text-partitioning node. The choice of the type of an index node depends on the spatial and textual distribution of the data objects. If the data objects have high spatial-overlap, then using a text-node to partition the data objects according to their textual components would be a better approach. Similarly, if the data objects share many keywords, then spatial partitioning would be a better partitioning approach. One limitation of the AP-tree is that it uses a variant of the ordered keyword trie that has high memory requirements. Also, the ordered keyword trie requires prior knowledge of the entire indexed vocabulary of keywords.

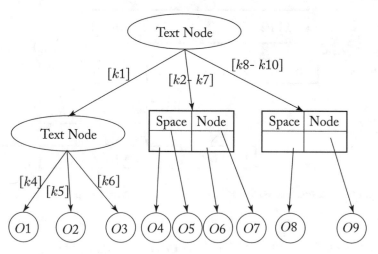

Figure 3.16: The AP-tree index.

FAST

FAST [79] is an interleaved spatial-keyword index that leverages the varying popularity of keywords across the different spatial regions to improve its processing performance while reducing its overall memory overhead.

FAST adopts a new text index, termed the Adaptive Keyword Index (AKI). FAST integrates AKI with the spatial pyramid structure [141]. AKI addresses the limitations of existing text indexes, mainly, the inverted list and the ordered keyword-trie. The inverted-list structure suffers from poor performance when having long posting-lists. The ordered keyword-trie has high memory-requirements. AKI starts as a ranked-key inverted-list structure as in Figure 3.17a, where all the data objects are indexed using a single keyword and all the keywords are considered infrequent. However, when the number of objects in a posting list of a specific keyword exceeds a specific threshold, this keyword is no longer considered infrequent. Data objects attached to frequent keywords do not get indexed using a single keyword, as illustrated in Figure 3.17b. In this figure, more keywords are used to distinguish the indexed data objects in a trie-like manner. The main advantage of this approach is that it applies high textual-discrimination only when needed. This results in reduced memory-overhead.

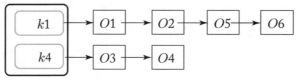

(a) Long Posting Lists in Ranked-Key Inverted Lists

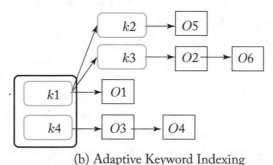

(b) Adaptive Keyword Indexing

Figure 3.17: The adaptive keyword index in FAST (AKI).

In FAST, AKI is integrated with a spatial pyramid, as illustrated in Figure 3.18. This integration adds spatial discrimination power when the indexed data objects cannot be textually discriminated any further, i.e., when AKI loses its textual discrimination power, e.g., when many data objects have the same set of keywords. These long lists are broken into smaller parts and descend to a lower pyramid-level with higher spatial-discrimination power. To reduce the overall memory requirements of FAST, cells of the spatial pyramid share lists of indexed objects while not affecting the search performance. One limitation of FAST is that it does not support rather complex spatial-keyword predicates, e.g., the spatial-keyword top-k select predicate.

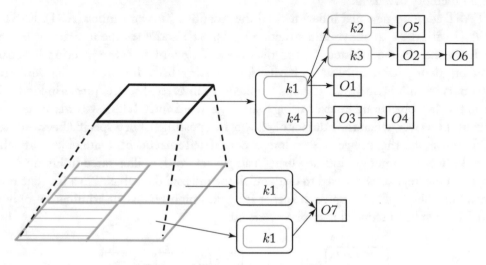

Figure 3.18: The interleaved structure of FAST.

3.3.4 SEPARATE SPATIAL AND KEYWORD INDEXES

In this approach, spatial-keyword data-objects are indexed using two separate indexes. One index is spatial, e.g., an R-tree, a spatial pyramid, or a quadtree. The other index is textual, e.g., an inverted list or an ordered-keyword-trie. Lee et al. [139] use separate spatial and keyword indexes to answer spatial-keyword queries. In this approach, a single spatial-keyword query is split into two sub-queries. The first sub-query is a spatial range query that is directed to the spatial index. This spatial sub-query filters the spatial-keyword data-objects that are indexed in the spatial index using only the spatial criteria. The second sub-query is a text query that is directed to the text index. This approach uses a query optimizer that builds a query plan based on an estimated selectivity of the underlying sub-queries. This query plan attempts to reduce the overall overhead needed to calculate the final result of answering spatial-keyword queries from multiple indexes.

3.3.5 SPATIOTEMPORAL-KEYWORD INDEXING

One specific class of centralized spatial-keyword indexes is the spatiotemporal-keyword index. Most spatial-keyword data objects have an associated timestamp, e.g., tweets and web searches. Having an index that accounts for the temporal attribute of the data helps answer queries that involve the time dimension. In this section, we present an example spatiotemporal-keyword index.

ST2I

ST2I [53] is a spatiotemporal-keyword index that is based on the kd-tree structure [158]. ST2I follows the partitioning approach used in the traditional kd-tree, where every level in ST2I is assigned to one attribute in the following repetitive order: time, longitude, latitude, text, time, etc. In every level in ST2I, a node is split at the median point of the indexed data. The median point for the time, longitude, and latitude dimensions can be calculated directly. However, for the text dimension, a special encoding function maps the strings of keywords into numbers. The splitting point of the text dimension is defined based on the median of the number representation of the encoded strings. Figure 3.19 illustrates the structure of the ST2I index. The main limitation of this index is that it does not support insertions or deletions. Moreover, it assumes only static data because it requires knowing, in advance, the median split point for each dimension.

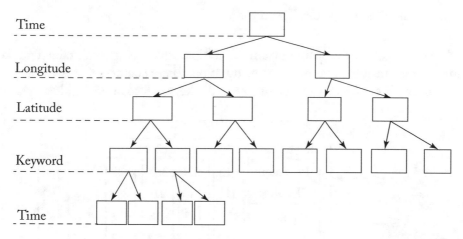

Figure 3.19: The architecture of ST2I [53].

3.4   CASE STUDIES

The proliferation of spatial-keyword data and its applications has resulted in the development of many centralized and distributed spatial-keyword data management systems (SKDMSs). In this section, we present examples of centralized systems that perform spatial-keyword processing.

GeoTrend

GeoTrend [88] is a centralized system that is designed to identify trending keywords of microblogs in any given location. GeoTrend answers the top-k frequent keywords query for any input spatial range. Figure 3.20 illustrates the structure of GeoTrend. GeoTrend uses a spatial pyramid to maintain hierarchical statistics about the trending keywords. Every cell in the spatial pyramid covers four child cells in the subsequent pyramid level (except for the leaf level). The statistics of the trending keywords in any pyramid cell at a specific level is the result of aggregating the statistics of the trending keywords in the child pyramid cells.

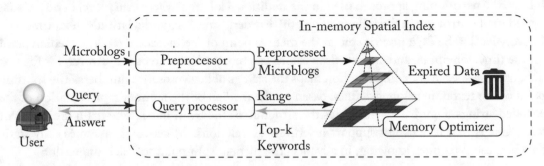

Figure 3.20: The architecture of GeoTrend [88].

Within every cell in the spatial pyramid, multiple counters are maintained per keyword. Each counter is responsible for a specific time duration. These counters represent the popularity of a keyword over time. Figure 3.21 demonstrates the keyword counters inside a pyramid cell.

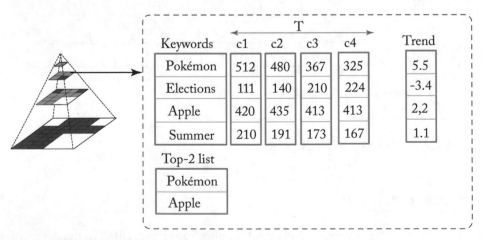

Figure 3.21: The counters of GeoTrend [88].

Every keyword within a pyramid cell is assigned a score that represents how frequent and trendy the keyword is. GeoTrend uses a memory optimizer module that keeps the most important data and statistics in main memory while purging extra data into disk. The preprocessor module in GeoTrend receives a stream of microblogs, and extracts relevant information, i.e., the timestamps, locations, and keywords of the streamed microblogs. The query processing module receives queries from users, and searches the spatial pyramid to provide the query results.

AFIA: The Adaptive Frequent-Item Aggregator

AFIA [97] is a centralized system for identifying the top-k frequent keywords in specific spatial ranges. Figure 3.22 illustrates the structure of AFIA. AFIA uses multi-level grids for spatial indexing (SI, for short). In every spatial grid-cell, counters about the frequent keywords are maintained, i.e., frequent-item counters (FIC, for short). AFIA does not maintain counters for all the keywords to reduce AFIA's memory requirements. AFIA maintains a temporal index (TI) to support querying the time dimension. Multiple instances of the spatial grid-cells are maintained to hold counters for the least supported time interval, e.g., one hour. Aggregate temporal cells are created to support coarser temporal granularities, e.g., days, weeks, and months. The steps for processing a top-k frequent keyword query are as follows: (1) identify the relevant spatial grid-cells based on the spatial range of the query; (2) collect counters from the spatial grid-cells; and (3) combine counters to produce the final result.

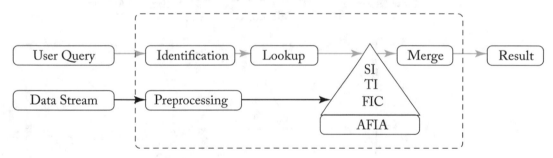

Figure 3.22: The architecture of AFIA [97].

SKYPE

SKYPE [96] is a system for answering continuous spatial-keyword top-k queries over a sliding window. The spatial-keyword top-k query has a point location and an associated set of keywords, and it is required to retrieve the k most-relevant spatial-keyword data objects. Relevance is based on a function of (1) the textual similarity between the object and the query and (2) the spatial distance between the location of the object and the location of the query. The main application of SKYPE is publish/subscribe processing, where subscribers register a continuous interest in the top-k relevant spatial-keyword messages, i.e., spatial-keyword data objects. In SKYPE, a tuple-based sliding-window is maintained. In the tuple-based sliding-window, the most recent w tuples are maintained.

SKYPE is structured into two main modules: (1) a message-dissemination module and (2) a top-k re-evaluation module. Refer to Figure 3.23 for illustration. The message-dissemination module contains a spatial-keyword index, termed the subscription index, that stores and maintains all the continuous top-k queries. The subscription index is a space-first spatial-keyword index that uses a quadtree for spatial indexing, where the leaf level of the quadtree contains an inverted list for textual indexing. The subscription index receives the incoming top-k queries, and removes the expired top-k queries. The incoming messages are directed to the subscription index to identify the continuous queries that are affected by an incoming spatial-keyword object. The top-k re-evaluation module uses an IR-tree [143] to maintain the most-recent w spatial-keyword objects. The most-recent w spatial-keyword objects are maintained to have the initial results to answer the incoming top-k spatial-keyword queries. Also, the top-k re-evaluation module maintains a *result buffer* that contains a set of top-k relevant objects for every continuous query. This result buffer gets updated in the following situations: (1) the arrival of new queries; (2) the expiry of existing queries; (3) the arrival of new spatial-keyword objects to be added into the sliding window; and (4) the expiry of spatial-keyword objects as they fall out of the sliding window. DSkype is a distributed version of SKYPE that is described in Section 4.2.2.

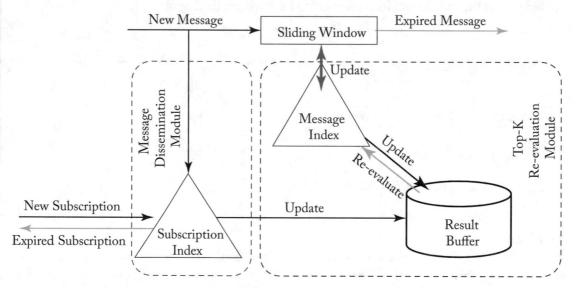

Figure 3.23: The architecture of SKYPE [96].

TwitterStand

TwitterStand [75, 176–178, 183] is a system for detecting and extracting news from tweets. Figure 3.24 illustrates the structure of TwitterStand. In TwitterStand, tweets are collected from multiple sources, e.g., the Twitter firehose [2], and by following users that are known to produce news. The collected tweets are classified to identify the tweets that potentially contain news. Then, the candidate tweets are clustered to group the tweets related to the same event. The tweets are geo-tagged to assign the detected news to specific spatial locations to be presented to users through a map-based interface.

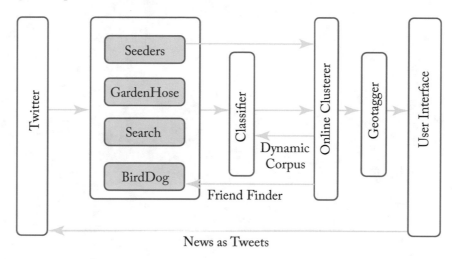

Figure 3.24: The architecture of TwitterStand [75].

CHAPTER 4

Distributed Spatial-Keyword Processing

Centralized spatial-keyword processing systems are limited in scale. They cannot handle the massive amounts of spatial-keyword data as they are restricted by the resources of the single machine they run on. The need for scalable processing of spatial-keyword data motivated the development of big SKDMS. The following are three main approaches for processing big spatial-keyword data.

1. Applications on top of general-purpose big-data systems, where the processing of spatial-keyword data takes place without any changes to the underlying big-data system.

2. Extensions to existing big-data systems, where the underlying big-data system is modified and is extended to be optimized for spatial-keyword processing.

3. Dedicated big spatial-keyword management systems, where big SKDMSs are built from scratch for the sole application of spatial-keyword processing.

In this chapter, we start with a brief overview of general-purpose big-data systems. Then, we present the main approaches for big spatial-keyword processing and indexing. Finally, we give examples and case studies on distributed systems that deal with spatial-keyword data.

4.1 GENERAL-PURPOSE BIG-DATA SYSTEMS

General-purpose big-data systems provide an infrastructure for processing data at scale. These general-purpose systems encapsulate main components of distributed processing, e.g., communication protocols among processes, reliability, fault tolerance, and process management. These components allow users of general-purpose big-data systems to focus on implementing the logic behind their applications. In general, these systems are not specifically optimized to process spatial-keyword data. There are two main types of general-purpose big-data systems: (1) batch-oriented systems and (2) streaming systems.

4.1.1 BATCH-ORIENTED SYSTEMS

Batch-oriented big-data systems, e.g., Hadoop [36] and Spark [14], process huge amounts of data in batches in an offline manner. Tasks running on batch-oriented systems require several minutes or even hours to finish the processing. Batch-oriented big-data systems are either disk-based, e.g., Hadoop [36], or memory-based, e.g., Spark [14, 105]. Processing of data is performed using one or more MapReduce jobs. Figure 4.1 illustrates the execution of a MapReduce job. Input data is split, and is fed into the mappers. The mappers perform specific processing over the input data to produce key-value pairs. Once the mapper phase terminates, the key-value pairs are sent to the reducers. Each reducer receives a batch of key-value pairs that are grouped by key, i.e., all key-value pairs with the same key are forwarded to the same reducer. Upon completing of the processing, reducers produce the final output. Many applications require running multiple consecutive MapReduce jobs, where the output of one MapReduce job is fed as input to the subsequent MapReduce job. In disk-based big-data systems, all the intermediate results of the consecutive MapReduce jobs are persisted on disk. However, in a memory-based system, intermediate results are kept in memory. This makes memory-based big-data systems more suitable for jobs that require multiple iterations over the data, e.g., linear regression [138].

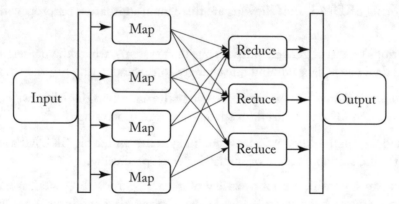

Figure 4.1: The execution model of a MapReduce system.

4.1.2   BIG-DATA STREAMING SYSTEMS

General-purpose big-data streaming systems enable the processing of continuous queries over rapidly arriving data streams. The main difference between batch-oriented systems and data streaming systems is that in a batch-oriented system, processing takes place on a snapshot of the data. However, in a data streaming system, data arrives progressively, and the results of a query are updated continuously as the new data arrives. There are two main types of big-data streaming systems:

1. tuple-based big-data streaming systems and

2. microbatch-based big-data streaming systems.

In a tuple-based big-data streaming system, e.g., Storm [87], Twitter Heron [57], and S4 [137], data tuples are processed as soon as they arrive with minimal processing latency. Figure 4.2 illustrates the structure of a general-purpose tuple-based big-data streaming system that has multiple data input nodes that are connected to a graph of worker nodes.

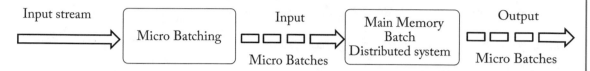

Figure 4.2: The structure of a general-purpose big-data streaming system.

In microbatch-based big-data streaming systems, e.g., Spark Streaming [106] and M3 [19], data tuples are grouped into small batches and processed every specific interval (or heartbeat as in M3), as illustrated in Figure 4.3. These systems often incur higher latency over tuple-based big-data streaming systems, e.g., the typical processing latency in Spark Streaming is one or two seconds.

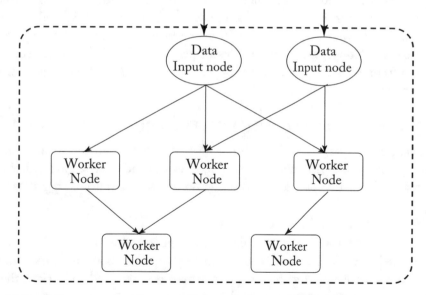

Figure 4.3: The execution model of microbatch-based streaming systems.

4.2 BIG SPATIAL-KEYWORD DATA MANAGEMENT SYSTEMS

General-purpose big-data systems are not equipped with the tools and the indexes needed to efficiently support spatial-keyword data. This lack of tools and tailored highly-optimized indexes have motivated the development of novel approaches for distributed spatial-keyword data processing. In this section, we study and categorize the main approaches for big spatial-keyword data processing. These approaches can be classified into the following three main categories:

1. applications on top of existing big-data systems,

2. extensions to general-purpose big-data systems, and

3. dedicated big SKDMSs.

Spatial-keyword applications on top of big-data systems do not change the structure of the underlying big-data system. The underlying big-data systems are not optimized toward spatial-keyword processing. This limits the performance of spatial-keyword applications. Dedicated big SKDMSs are designed to run specific spatial-keyword applications. These systems are highly optimized toward specific spatial-keyword use cases. However, dedicated systems cannot handle other processing types. This restricts the usage of these dedicated big SKDMSs. General-purpose big-data systems can be modified and extended to handle spatial-keyword applications. One important extension to general-purpose big-data systems is spatial-keyword indexing. These extended big-data systems maintain their ability to handle general-purpose processing. Also, these extended systems achieve superior performance for spatial-keyword processing when compared to unextended systems. In this section, we give a detailed description of these approaches using several examples.

4.2.1 APPLICATION ON TOP OF EXISTING BIG-DATA SYSTEM

In this approach, a query-specific algorithm is designed to run on top of a general-purpose big-data system. The underlying big-data system does not incur any changes. Below, we give examples of spatial-keyword applications running on top general-purpose big-data systems.

Boolean kNN Processing on MapReduce

Li et al. [60] propose a MapReduce-based algorithm to process the boolean k-Nearest-Neighbor query over spatial-keyword data that is stored in Hadoop. The Boolean kNN query is a special version of the spatial-keyword top-k query, where it is required to retrieve the k-nearest spatial-keyword data objects that contain all the query keywords. The map phase of the algorithm extracts the spatial-keyword attributes of the data objects. Based on these attributes, the spatial-keyword data objects are checked to determine whether or not they contain all the query keywords. During the map phase, the distances between the location of the query and the locations of all the qualified spatial-keyword objects are calculated. In the reduce phase, spatial-keyword data objects are partitioned and are sorted based on their distances to the location of the query. At the end of the reduce phase, the k-nearest data objects are returned as the query result. Figure 4.4 illustrates the MapReduce algorithm for processing of the Boolean kNN query.

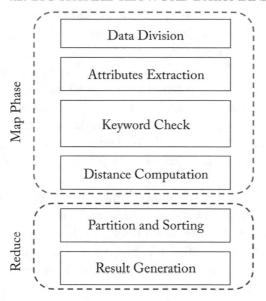

Figure 4.4: The MapReduce algorithm for evaluating the Boolean kNN query.

Spatial-Keyword Group Query-Processing on Graphs

The m-closest keyword (mCK) query is an important spatial-keyword query that identifies a group of spatial-keyword objects that are very close to each other and that collectively cover the query keywords. Finding an optimal answer to the mCK query is an NP-Hard problem. Hao et al. [51] present a MapReduce-based algorithm for finding an approximate answer to the mCK query over a road network. The algorithm gives an approximate answer by searching for *group Steiner-trees* in the road network graph. A group Steiner-tree is a tree whose nodes represent spatial-keyword data objects. The nodes of a group Steiner-tree should collectively cover the query keywords. The edges of the group Steiner tree are edges of the road network with minimal overall edge-weight. The algorithm goes through two phases: (1) an offline partitioning phase and (2) an online MapReduce search phase. In the offline partitioning phase, the road-network graph of the spatial-keyword data objects is partitioned into subgraphs. Since a group Steiner-tree may span multiple partitions, some partitions are extended to contain edges from other partitions to ensure that any group Steiner-tree is found within at least one partition. This results in an overlapped partitioning of the spatial-keyword data. The MapReduce search phase scans the partitions of the road network to identify all candidate group Steiner-trees. Then, the candidate group Steiner-trees are ranked to find the one with minimum overall edge-weight.

Spatial-Keyword kNN-Join over Wireless Sensor Networks

Monitoring of the environment using Wireless Sensor Networks (WSNs) can be regarded as a spatial-keyword application, where the locations of sensors constitute the spatial data and the description of the events monitored by the WSN constitute the textual data. For example, in military applications, WSNs are deployed at many locations to sense the existence of hostile activities, e.g., tanks or walking armories.

The spatial-keyword kNN-join query is formulated as a set of keywords and a set of locations and for every location, say l, it is required to retrieve the K-nearest sensor nodes to l that contain all the query keywords. For example, soldiers may issue a query to retrieve the k-nearest tanks to them. The main challenge in processing spatial-keyword queries in WSNs is the limited computational and power resources of the WSNs nodes. Yang et al. [104] present a technique to offload the processing of the spatial-keyword kNN-join query from WSNs nodes to a Hadoop MapReduce-cluster.

The processing on the Hadoop cluster goes through two phases: (1) a preprocessing phase and (2) a query-processing phase. In the preprocessing phase, an inverted-list index is built on top of the textual description of all the sensor nodes. In the query-processing phase, a MapReduce job is issued the identify the candidate WSNs nodes that contain the query keywords using the inverted-list index. Then, for every location, say l, the k-nearest sensor-nodes are identified in the reduce phase.

4.2.2   EXTENSION TO GENERAL-PURPOSE BIG-DATA SYSTEMS

Executing query-specific algorithms on top of general-purpose big-data systems does not provide the best utilization of the resources of the underlying big-data system. The reason is that the general-purpose big-data systems are not inherently optimized for spatial-keyword data indexing, e.g., these systems are not equipped with spatial-keyword workload partitioning and indexing techniques. To address this issue, several extensions to general-purpose big-data systems have been proposed. These extensions make big-data systems aware of the spatial and the textual attributes of the data. This significantly improves the performance of these extended systems when handling spatial-keyword data and spatial-keyword processing queries. Below, we present example spatial-keyword extensions to general-purpose big-data systems.

Tornado

Tornado [71, 152] is a distributed spatial-keyword data streaming system that extends Storm [87], an open-source general-purpose distributed data streaming system. The main idea behind Tornado is to extend Storm with the following two new layers: (1) an adaptive routing layer and (2) a spatial-keyword evaluation layer. The adaptive routing layer uses a spatial-keyword data structure that distributes relevant spatial-keyword data and queries to the same worker process. The spatial-keyword evaluation layer extends the worker processes of Storm with internal spatial-keyword indexing to store continuous queries. The routing layer in Tornado is able to detect changes in the distribution of the workload by periodically collecting workload statistics from the distributed worker processes. If a worker process becomes under high workload, the overall throughput of the system may be affected. In this case, the routing layer re-adjusts the distribution of the workload to alleviate this bottleneck and to eventually restore the performance of the system. Figure 4.5 illustrates the structure of Tornado. Details of the indexing techniques used inside Tornado are presented in Section 3.3.3.

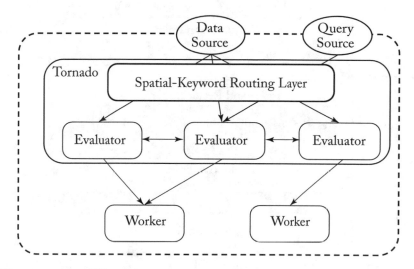

Figure 4.5: The structure of Tornado.

DSkype

DSkype [95] is a distributed spatial-keyword data streaming system that extends Storm [87]. DSkype is a distributed version of the SKYPE index described in Section 3.4. Skype answers the continuous version of the spatial-keyword top-k query in a centralized setting. A continuous top-k spatial-keyword query has a point location and an associated set of keywords. It is required to continuously report the top-k relevant spatial-keyword objects. The main application for DSkype is publish/subscribe [70] processing, where continuous queries represent subscriptions while spatial-keyword data represent published messages. Figure 4.6 illustrates the structure of the DSkype system. In this figure, the term *bolt* refers to a worker process in Storm. DSkype has specific workload distribution bolts, i.e., processes. These distribution bolts receive continuous queries (also referred to as subscriptions), and forward these queries to subscription bolts that are designated for storing and processing the continuous queries. The incoming spatial-keyword data are distributed through the distribution bolts to the subscription bolts to update the results of the relevant continuous queries. Also, the same incoming spatial-keyword data is forwarded to another set of data bolts (termed the message bolts) to store a limited history of the messages. The limited history provides the initial answer to the newly arriving continuous spatial-keyword queries.

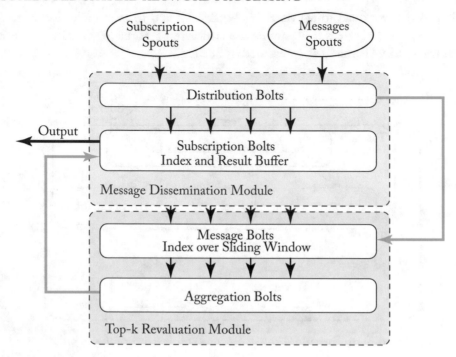

Figure 4.6: The architecture of DSkype [95].

PS2Stream

PS2Stream [153] is an adaptive and a distributed data streaming system that extends Storm [87]. PS2Stream answers a continuous version of the spatial-keyword filter query. The main application for PS2Stream is publish/subscribe processing, where users submit continuous queries as subscriptions with specific spatial ranges and keywords. For the incoming spatial-keyword data, it is required to identify the matching continuous queries. PS2Stream is structured into three layers (refer to Figure 4.7 for illustration): (1) dispatchers, (2) workers, and (3) mergers. Dispatchers receive the incoming spatial-keyword data and continuous queries, and distribute them to the Workers. Workers maintain spatial-keyword indexes for indexing the continuous queries. Mergers are responsible for aggregating the results from multiple workers. PS2Stream is adaptive to workload changes, where it redistributes the data and query workloads to workers according to changes in the distribution of data and/or queries.

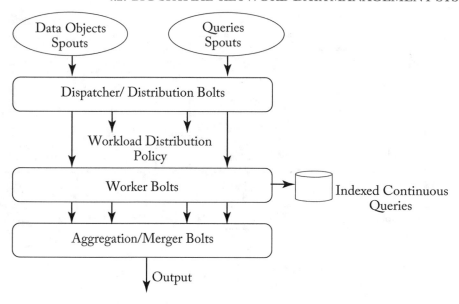

Figure 4.7: The architecture of PS2Stream [153].

4.2.3   DEDICATED BIG SPATIAL-KEYWORD DATA MANAGEMENT SYSTEMS

Dedicated big SKDMSs are designed with the sole objective of handling specific spatial-keyword applications. Thus, these dedicated systems are not for generic use beyond their specified application. In the following, we give examples of dedicated big SKDMSs.

NewsStand

NewsStand [78, 181, 183–192] is a system for news aggregation and geo-tagging. NewsStand ensures the distributed processing of data by separating the data collection modules from the data processing modules and having them run independently. Instances of these modules can run independently in a distributed cluster. The data collection modules use *distributed* news crawlers to collect news documents from the Web and to store the documents in a core database. The processing module geo-tags the collected web pages and then clusters them based on their locations to eventually associate news pages to their relevant locations. Figure 4.8 illustrates the interactions between the modules of NewsStand.

TAGHREED

TAGHREED [146] is a system for the analysis of microblogs. The system consists of three main modules: (1) the query engine, (2) the indexer, and (3) the recovery manager. The query engine receives and optimizes the incoming queries over microblogs. The indexer keeps the most

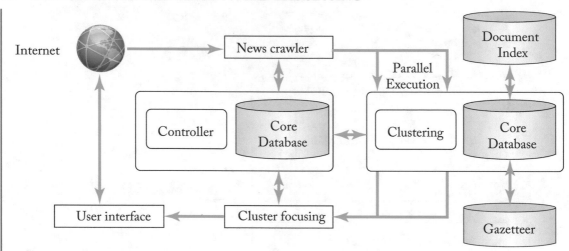

Figure 4.8: The architecture of NewsStand [78].

relevant tweets in main-memory, and uses a flushing mechanism to evict tweets that are not likely to contribute to the query results. TAGHREED contains a recovery manager to restore the system in case of failures. Figure 4.9 illustrates the structure of TAGHREED. TAGHREED mainly supports filtering queries that filter tweets based on their spatial, temporal, and textual attributes. To support a wider range of queries, TAGHREED uses *distributed* processes, termed distributed data scanner, to refine results according to additional attributes other than the ones above. Section 4.3.3 presents an overview of the indexing techniques adopted in TAGHREED.

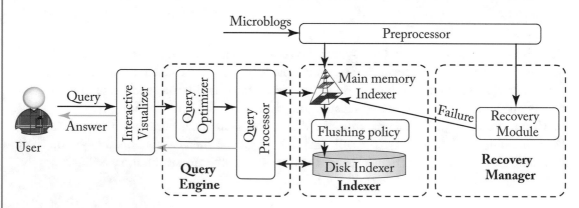

Figure 4.9: The architecture of TAGHREED [146].

4.3   STRATEGIES TO DISTRIBUTE AND INDEX DATA IN BIG SKDMSS

Big SKDMSs adopt various types of indexing techniques to improve their performance. Indexes in big SKDMSs account for the distributed nature of the underlying system. In big SKDMSs, data is often split into smaller blocks or partitions. Most indexes in big spatial-keyword management systems use a two-layered approach that is composed of a top-layer and a lower-layer. The top-layer (also termed the global index) identifies the relevant data partitions for a given query or operation. The lower-layer (also termed the local indexes) indexes the data inside a specific partition. This two-layered model is applicable to both the batch-oriented and streaming systems. Indexing approaches in big SKDMSs can be classified into the following three categories:

1. spatial-only indexing,

2. hash-based indexing, and

3. hybrid indexing.

The following sections cover each of these indexing categories for SKDMSs.

4.3.1   SPATIAL-ONLY INDEXING

This simplistic approach uses a spatial-only data structure for indexing spatial-keyword data. To answer spatial-keyword queries, the spatial predicate of the query is used. Textual predicates are applied on the fly as a post-processing step. We present one example of a spatial-only indexing technique for big SKDMSs.

TAREEG
TAREEG [26] is a service for extracting spatial-keyword features from map data, e.g., road networks, lakes, and rivers. TAREEG runs on top of SpatialHadoop [28]. SpatialHadoop is a big spatial-only data management system that extends Hadoop MapReduce [36]. TAREEG answers the spatial-keyword filter query on top of map data, e.g., OpenStreetMap [3]. Indexing in TAREEG is spatial-only and inherits the two-layered spatial index from SpatialHadoop. Figure 4.10 illustrates the spatial indexes in TAREEG. The top-layer, i.e., the global index, of the spatial index uses either grid-based or R-tree-based partitioning of the indexed data. The lower-layer, i.e., the local indexes, uses grid-based or R-tree-based indexing of spatial data. In SpatialHadoop, the top-layer partitioning and the lower-layer indexing are of the same type, i.e., both are either grid-based or are both R-tree-based. The structure of TAREEG is illustrated in Figure 4.11. Queries directed to TAREEG use the spatial indexes inside SpatialHadoop to identify data that is spatially relevant to the spatial-keyword filter query. The query processor applies the textual filter on the fly before returning the query results to users.

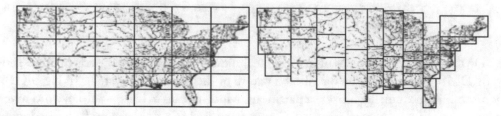

Figure 4.10: Grid-based and R-tree-based indexing in TAREEG. Based on [26].

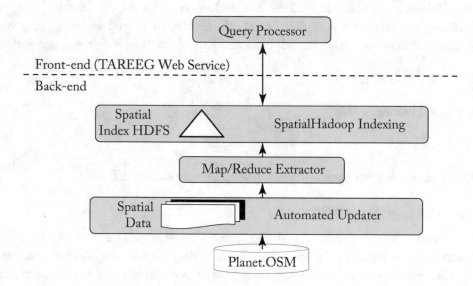

Figure 4.11: The architecture of TAREEG [26].

4.3.2   HASH-BASED INDEXING

This spatial-keyword indexing approach depends mainly on using a hash table. The key to the hash table is an encoding of the spatial and textual properties of the indexed data. In what follows, we give two examples of hash-based spatial-keyword indexing in big SKDMSs.

Keyword Geocoding for Top-k Local User Search

Jiang et al. [55] realize a big SKDMS for answering the *top-k local-users query* over microblogs, i.e., tweets. This query type identifies the users that produce the most popular and widespread tweets for specific spatial locations. The popularity of a user depends on the number of replies and shares the user gets for his/her tweets. The top-k local users can be seen as the local experts in their surrounding locations. This system stores tweets in Hadoops's Distributed File System (HDFS) [76]. To speed up query processing, this system uses an inverted-list-based index on tweets. The inverted-list index is illustrated in Figure 4.12. The tweets are indexed, and are stored in HDFS. This index has two layers: (1) a forward index and (2) an inverted index. The forward index resides in main-memory, and is basically a hash table. The key to the hash table is $< geo, kw >$, where geo is a geo-hash value that is calculated by assigning objects to nodes of a quadtree, and kw is a keyword that exists in the indexed tweets. To calculate the geo-hash geo, every node in the quadtree has an encoding that is either 00, 01, 10, or 11, and this depends on the quadrant of the node, i.e., whether it is the top-left, top-right, bottom-left, or bottom-right quadrant. A leaf-level quadtree node has a geo-hash that concatenates the signature of all the quadtree nodes on the path from this leaf node to the root. The key to the hash table in the forward index concatenates the geo-hash of a quadtree node with the keywords that exist in that node. Every entry in the forward index has a pointer to a posting list in the inverted index that is stored in HDFS. The posting lists of the inverted index contain lists of pointers to tweets that are stored in HDFS, as illustrated in Figure 4.12.

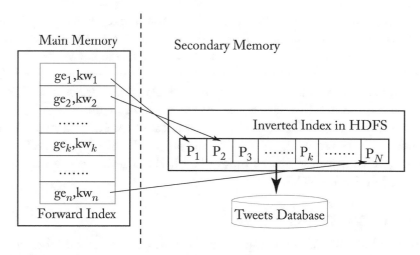

Figure 4.12: Hash-based inverted indexing for top-k local user search [55].

STbHI: Spatial- and Textual-Based Hybrid Index in ST-HBase

Spatio-Textual HBase (ST-HBase) [66] is a system that extends HBase [100]. HBase is an open-source key-value data store realized on top of the Hadoop Distributed File System (HDFS) [76] that supports the execution of SQL-like queries. ST-HBase improves the performance of the spatial-keyword filter query by introducing spatial-keyword indexing. The *Spatial- and Textual-Based Hybrid Index (STbHI)* is a hash-based index in ST-HBase. When storing data in an HBase table, a key for every row is needed. In HBase, queries on row keys are executed efficiently. STbHI organizes data in HBase tables using a spatial-keyword row key. The row key is calculated using a concatenation of keywords and the z-ordering value of the spatial location of the indexed objects, as illustrated in Figure 4.13. In this figure, the row key of the first tuple in the table is the concatenation of one keyword term $t1$ from the object identified by id_1.

Rowkey	id	x	y
$t_1$0101101	id_1	x_1	y_1
$t_2$0101001	id_2	x_2	y_2
$t_3$0110101	id_1	x_1	y_1
$t_3$1100111	id_3	x_3	y_3

Inverted Index Table Schema

Figure 4.13: STbHI: Spatial- and Textual-based Hybrid Index in ST-HBase [66].

To answer a spatial-keyword filter query, the spatial range of the query is mapped into a set of z-ordered values with maximum resolution (i.e., as a set of points coded by their z-ordered values). These z-ordered values are concatenated with the keywords of the query. This approach is efficient for queries with small spatial ranges. However, queries with large spatial ranges have many search keys that come from the calculated z-order values. This reduces the query performance because ST-HBase tables are searched with multiple keys. Also, in this indexing approach, every spatial-keyword object is replicated for every keyword in the object's textual attribute as illustrated in Figure 4.13 for the object identified by id_1. ST-HBase adopts the Term Cluster-based Inverted Spatial Index (TCbISI) to alleviate the limitations of STbHI. TCbISI is studied in Section 4.3.3.

4.3.3 HYBRID INDEXING

Hybrid indexes in big SKDMSs integrate a spatial index and a textual index to improve the execution of spatial-keyword queries. In this section, we study several hybrid indexes that are used in big SKDMSs.

TCbISI: Term Cluster-Based Inverted Spatial Index in ST-HBase
ST-HBase [66] adopts TCbISI to overcome the limitation of STbHI (refer to Section 4.3.2). TCbISI is a hybrid index that integrates the kd-tree spatial index [158], inverted lists, and clustering, to optimize the execution of the spatial-keyword filter query in ST-HBase. TCbISI clusters keywords that co-occur frequently into *term clusters*. This clustering of keywords addresses the main limitation of STbHI that requires a replica of the indexed objects for every keyword contained in the objects. TCbISI's storage requirements are lower than those of STbHI. An inverted list is realized for every keyword to associate the keyword with a term cluster. The objects within the term clusters are spatially indexed using a kd-tree [158]. The leaf-level of the kd-tree points to the indexed objects in HBase. Figure 4.14 illustrates the organization of the

TCbISI index. Spatial-keyword filter queries are executed by first checking the inverted list to identify the relevant term clusters. Then, the kd-trees of relevant term clusters are queried using the spatial predicates of the query to identify the relevant spatial-keyword objects in the storage of HBase.

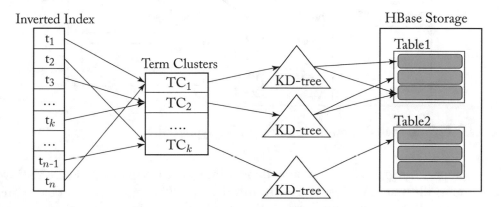

Figure 4.14: TCbISI: Term Cluster-based Inverted Spatial Index [66].

DSkype

DSkype [95] is a big SKDMS for answering continuous top-k spatial-keyword queries over a sliding window. DSkype is realized on top of Storm [87], a general purpose distributed data stream management system. DSkype uses the two-layered model for indexing continuous queries and maintaining a sliding window over spatial-keyword data. The top-layer of the index distributes the incoming continuous queries to multiple worker processes. The worker processes store the continuous top-k queries, and contain the local-layer of the spatial-keyword index. The local index in DSKype is a hybrid index that integrates a quadtree with an inverted-list structure to store the continuous top-k queries. Every node in the quadtree contains an inverted list of queries that are stored in this node. Figure 4.15 illustrates the structure of the hybrid local index in DSKype.

Hybrid Indexing in Spark

He et al. [52] propose a hybrid spatial-keyword index in Spark [14]. This hybrid index is designed to optimize the execution of a specific instance of the spatial-keyword ranked-group query described in Section 2.1.3. This version of the spatial-keyword ranked-group query has a focal point and an associated set of keywords. It is required to retrieve a group of spatial-keyword objects that collectively cover the query keywords and optimizes a spatial cost-function. The spatial cost-function depends on two factors: (1) the distance between the location of the query focal point and the group and (2) the total distances between each two of the objects in the group,

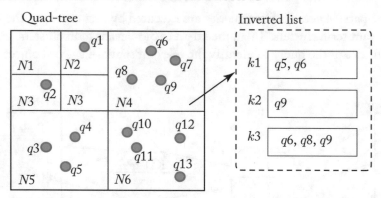

Figure 4.15: Hybrid spatial-keyword indexing in DSKype [66].

i.e., how compact the group is. The proposed index integrates the spatial grid with the inverted list structure as illustrated in Figure 4.16. In this figure, spatial-keyword data objects are first partitioned spatially using the spatial grid index. Then, for every keyword in the vocabulary of indexed objects, an inverted list of the grid cells containing the keyword is maintained. Objects belonging to the same spatial grid-cell are stored in the same HDFS block. Every spatial grid-cell maintains pointers to the relevant HDFS blocks.

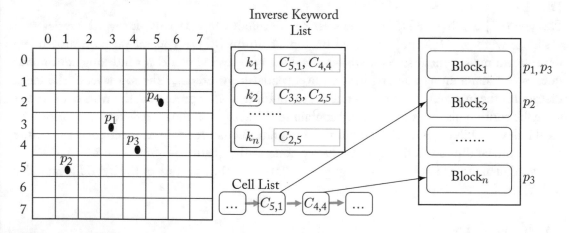

Figure 4.16: Hybrid spatial-keyword indexing in Spark [52].

To answer the collective spatial-keyword group query, we need to identify the relevant spatial grid cells. A relevant spatial grid-cell is a cell that contains objects whose textual description overlaps the query keywords. The search for relevant grid-cells begins at the grid cell that contains the focal point of the query. The search range increases in a spiral way until all the query keywords are covered by the current set of candidate grid-cells. Any grid cell that does not have any keywords that overlap the query keywords is excluded. The objective of this inverted list is to minimize the number of grid cells being searched when answering the collective spatial-keyword group-query. Then, the data objects in the candidate grid-cells are processed to provide the final answer to the collective spatial-keyword group query.

TAGHREED

TAGHREED [146] is a microblogs management system outlined in Section 4.2.3. TAGHREED answers spatial-keyword queries with spatial-range predicates, textual predicates, and a temporal predicate. All queries answered by TAGHREED need to have a specific time-range. TAGHREED uses a variation of the two-layered indexing model. The adopted model uses a main-memory layer and a disk-resident layer. The main idea behind TAGHREED is that the incoming queries are more likely to search the recent microblogs. The microblogs in recent-time ranges are indexed in main-memory. Periodically, the non-relevant microblogs are flushed from main-memory to disk. This flushing frees the main-memory to hold the newly incoming microblogs. Also, the flushed microblogs are indexed in the disk-resident layer of TAGHREED. Figure 4.17 illustrates the main-memory indexing layer of TAGHREED. In this layer, both the spatial pyramid and the inverted index are used to index the microblogs. These separate spatial and textual indexes are segmented, where every index segment (spatial or textual) is responsible for a specific temporal range. This segmentation eases the flushing of the non-relevant microblogs to disk. Also, this improves query processing, and speeds up the data indexing process. In the disk-resident layer of TAGHREED, separate spatial and textual indexes are used. An R-tree is used as the spatial index while an inverted list is used as the textual index. The R-tree that is better suited for disk-based indexing over the spatial-pyramid index. Figure 4.18 illustrates the organization of the disk-based spatial indexing in TAGHREED. The disk-based spatial index is also segmented into non-overlapping temporal ranges, i.e., days, weeks, and months. A similar organization is adopted for the textual index. In TAGHREED, all the queries must have a temporal range. TAGHREED uses this temporal range to identify and search all the temporally overlapping indexes (the spatial and textual memory-resident and disk-resident indexes) to evaluate the final query answer.

4.3.4   PARTITIONING OF SPATIAL-KEYWORD DATA STREAMS

In streamed big SKDMSs, multiple worker processes receive, process, and send spatial-keyword data. One important aspect in streamed big SKDMSs is how to efficiently distribute the data and query workloads to the distributed worker nodes. In this section, we overview several techniques for partitioning spatial-keyword data streams.

Tornado

Tornado [71, 152] is a distributed spatial-keyword stream processing system that extends the Storm data streaming system [87]. The overall structure of Tornado is outlined in Section 4.2.2.

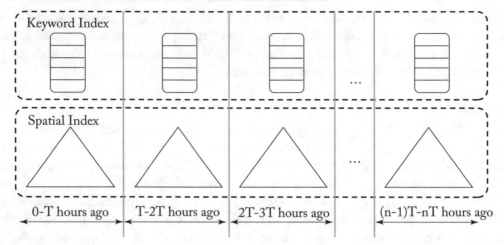

Figure 4.17: Main-memory indexing in TAGHREED [146].

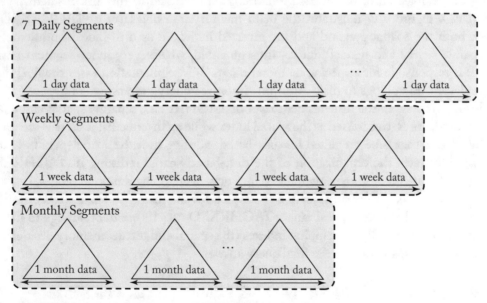

Figure 4.18: Disk-based indexing in TAGHREED [146].

Tornado uses a two-layered indexing approach as illustrated in Figure 4.19. The top index-layer in Tornado is termed the routing layer. In Tornado, the routing layer partitions the space into non-overlapping rectangles. Every rectangle is assigned to a worker node, i.e., an evaluator process as illustrated in Figure 4.20. This spatial partitioning is initialized using historical data. The routing layer maintains a summary of all the keywords of the queries being evaluated. This summary is used as a filter to prevent irrelevant spatial-keyword data objects from being routed when there are no queries interested in any of the keywords in these data objects. The spatial partitioning in the routing layer is adaptive to changes in the data and query workloads within the evaluators. The routing layer receives workload statistics from the evaluators, and re-adjusts the boundaries of the partitions accordingly while maintaining the correct execution of the continuous queries. The evaluators in Tornado uses the FAST spatial-keyword index [79]. FAST is described in Section 3.3.3.

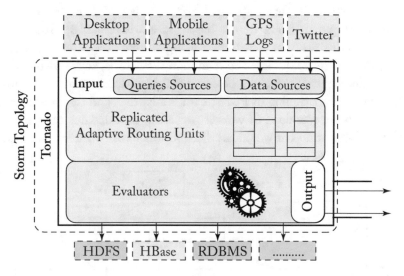

Figure 4.19: The architecture of Tornado [71, 152].

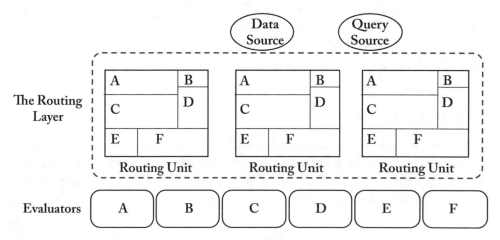

Figure 4.20: The routing layer of Tornado [71, 152].

PS2Stream

PS2Stream [153] is a distributed spatial-keyword data streaming system that is tailored toward the spatial-keyword filter query. Spatial-keyword indexing in PS2Stream is two-layered. The top-layer in PS2Stream distributes the incoming data and queries to multiple worker processes. The lower-layer in PS2stream uses a hybrid spatial-first index that integrates a spatial grid with an inverted list.

The top-layer partitioning technique in PS2Stream is illustrated in Figure 4.21. This approach uses spatial-first partitioning that is based on a kd-tree [158]. The incoming spatial-keyword data and queries are first partitioned using the kd-tree. Then, when certain spatial ranges in the leaf level of the spatial kd-tree span many keywords, keyword-based partitioning is applied. Thus, the same spatial range can be covered by multiple worker nodes that handle different sets of keywords. Partitioning in PS2Stream is adaptive, and the top-layer of PS2Stream continuously monitors the workload of worker processes, and updates the structure of the kd-tree-based indexes to maintain fair workload distribution across worker processes.

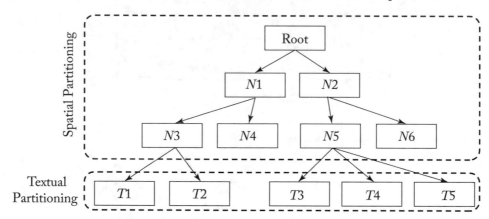

Figure 4.21: The global index in PS2stream [153].

4.4   CASE STUDIES

In this section, we present an overview of additional systems that deal with big spatial-keyword data. These systems may not be directly answering spatial-keyword queries. However, these systems perform relevant operations that contribute to spatial-keyword data management, e.g., building spatial-keyword indexes.

Disks

Disks [64, 65] is a distributed system for processing one variation of the spatial-keyword group query over road networks. This query identifies a group of spatial-keyword objects that are within a specific road-network distance from each other, and that collectively cover the query keywords.

Disks partitions the indexed road network into non-overlapping partitions. Each partition has a set of portal nodes that have edges to other partitions. Then, Disks builds an index within every partition, this index maintains distances between nodes and some portal nodes within the partition. This index is constructed using Hadoop MapReduce. Also, Disks maintains an inverted index that stores, for every keyword, the set of road-network nodes that contain this keyword. The spatial-keyword group query is executed in the following steps: (1) for every keyword, the inverted index is probed to identify the set of nodes that contain this keyword; (2) the indexes that are within each partition are used to identify the candidate groups of nodes that cover all the keywords, and that satisfy the distance threshold; and (3) the candidate groups of nodes are later intersected to identify the final query result. Query processing in Disks is performed using Hadoop MapReduce, where distributed processes operate over distributed partitions. Figure 4.22 illustrates the architecture of Disks and the steps for spatial-keyword indexing and query processing using Hadoop MapReduce.

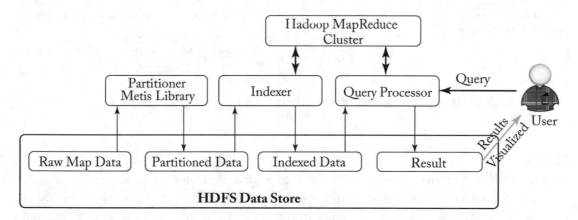

Figure 4.22: The structure of the Disks system [64, 65].

TerraFly sksOpen

TerraFly [108] is a system for querying and visualizing spatial and spatial-keyword data. TerraFly handles map requests and queries from over 125 countries. TerraFly supports multiple map-layers including street names, roads, restaurants, services, and demographic data. sksOpen [63] is an indexing and a querying engine inside TerraFly to answer the spatial-keyword top-k query. To efficiently answer the spatial-keyword top-k query, sksOpen builds a hybrid spatial-keyword index that integrates the R-tree with inverted lists. Notice that sksOpen does not integrate a spatial-keyword index into a general-purpose big-data system to become a big SKDMS. However, it uses a general-purpose big-data system to build a centralized spatial-keyword index. sksOpen uses Hadoop MapReduce to optimize the time needed to build a hybrid spatial-keyword index. The index is built in parallel, where data is partitioned spatially. A sub-index for each partition is built in the map phase. Then, these sub-indexes are merged into a single index in the reduce phase. Figure 4.23 illustrates the process for building the spatial-keyword index using Hadoop MapReduce.

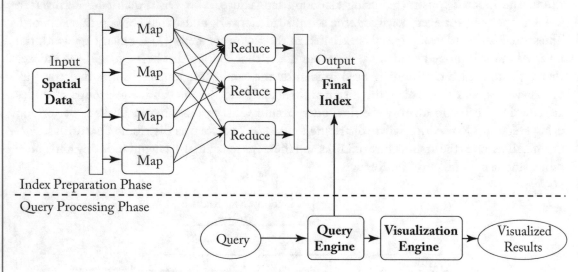

Figure 4.23: The structure of TerraFly sksOpen system [63, 108].

Nimbus

Nimbus [58] is a service for tuning the predicates used in twitter analysis. Nimbus attempts to assess the selectivity of the spatial-keyword query predicates over tweets by applying the analysis predicates on small sets of spatial-keywords. For example, when searching for tweets talking about "Adobe Photoshop," using the keyword "Photoshop" only may result in many irrelevant results. Nimbus uses a MySQL database to store a subset of the tweets to assess the selectivity of the incoming spatial-keyword queries over the stored dataset. Figure 4.24 illustrates the structure of the Nimbus system. It supports spatial-keyword processing by using the GNIP powertrack [4] query language that supports representing both spatial and textual predicates. Nimbus uses SparkStreaming [106] to ingest and process the incoming tweets, and to update the MySQL database with the new batches of tweets. Nimbus uses Spark [14] as a parallel evaluation environment to evaluate the quality of the predicates of queries against the stored dataset.

ModiSENSE

ModiSENSE [73] is a platform for discovering points of interest and trending events from social media and microblogs. This system integrates HBase [100] as a component of its storage layer and the Hadoop MapReduce [36] as the processing platform. The structure of ModiSENSE is

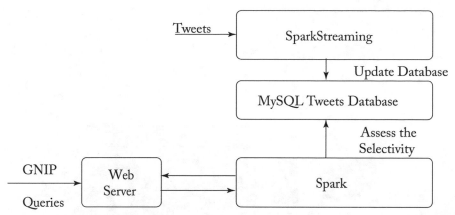

Figure 4.24: The structure of Nimbus system [58].

illustrated in Figure 4.25. HBase is used for executing batch queries that do not require real-time processing and for storing the newly arriving data, e.g., the GPS logs of users. PostgreSQL is used to store data that needs to be queried frequently and does not have frequent updates, e.g., the users' blogs. Event detection is performed using a MapReduce implementation of the DBScan clustering algorithm. This clustering algorithm runs on the GPS logs to detect high-density locations that can be potential points of interest.

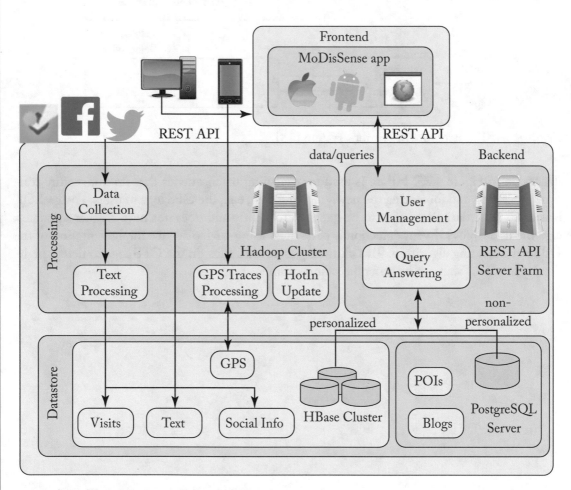

Figure 4.25: The structure of ModiSENSE. Used with permission.

CHAPTER 5

Open Research Problems in Spatial-Keyword Processing

The increasing demand for processing and analyzing massive amounts of spatial-keyword data poses new research challenges in the scalability, adaptivity, and expressibility of SKDMSs. In this chapter, we highlight and discuss some of the important research challenges.

5.1 LOAD BALANCING

Spatial-keyword data contains two main attributes: (1) the spatial attribute represented by the locations of the data objects and (2) the textual attribute represented by a set of keywords. In most spatial-keyword applications, it is extremely rare to have spatial-keyword data that is uniformly distributed across space. Similarly, for the textual attribute, the frequencies of keywords do not follow a uniform distribution. Instead, spatial-keyword data exhibits skewed spatial and textual distributions. In big SKDMSs, spatial-keyword data and queries are often partitioned across multiple processes. Workload partitioning mechanisms need to be aware of these skewed distributions to ensure load balancing among the participating worker processes. One important challenge when dealing with skewed spatial-keyword data is that the underlying spatial and textual distributions change over time. For example, Figure 5.1 gives a heat-map of the tweets talking about sunshine at different times of the day. This figure demonstrates that the spatial and textual distributions of tweets vary over time. The continuous variability and skewness of spatial-keyword distribution call for the development of adaptive big SKDMSs that react to changes in the workload to continuously ensure fair workload distribution and load balancing.

Existing adaptive SKDMSs are either designed for big spatial-only processing, e.g., AQWA [27], or address streamed spatial-keyword data for a restricted set of queries, e.g., Tornado [71, 152] and PS2Stream [153] that only consider the continuous spatial-keyword filter query. The lack of comprehensive SKDMSs calls for the design and development of novel adaptivity protocols that consider both batch and streaming environments for a wide range of spatial-keyword queries.

5.2 SPATIAL-KEYWORD BENCHMARKS

Benchmarking is the process of evaluating the performance of a system or device against a set of predefined test scenarios that target certain properties or aspects of the system or device being

(a) Morning Time in the East Coast
of the United States

(b) Night Time in the East Coast
of the United States

Figure 5.1: Geo-tagged tweets talking about sunshine at different times in the day. Based on [10].

benchmarked. When developing new spatial-keyword systems, it is important to have a benchmark that is able to assess the performance and the scalability of the system under different data and query workloads. Currently, there exist many benchmarks that evaluate the performance of spatial-only systems, e.g., [24, 25, 72]. BerlinMod [25] is a spatial-only benchmark that generates locations of moving objects over road networks as illustrated in Figure 5.2. Also, there exist relational-only benchmarks, e.g., TPC-H [8]. However, there exist few spatial-keyword benchmarks that only consider a limited set of spatial-keyword queries. For example, the benchmark

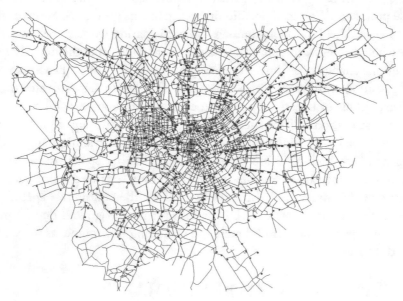

Figure 5.2: A sample snapshot of BerlinMOD data plotted on the map of Berlin city. Based on [77].

introduced by Chen et al. [125] propose a benchmark that evaluates the performance of spatial-keyword indexes under three spatial-keyword queries. Doudali et al. [44] propose a benchmark that focuses on evaluating data mining techniques for identifying patterns of interactions among users of social networks. The lack of a standard benchmark calls for the development of comprehensive spatial-keyword benchmarks that include large datasets and various realistic queries. An effective benchmark should consider both the batch-oriented and streaming scenarios. This benchmark is essential for the effective evaluation of emerging big SKDMSs.

5.3   SPATIAL-KEYWORD QUERY OPTIMIZER

Most existing SKDMSs handle small sets of spatial-keyword queries. These systems often answer these queries by introducing query-specific indexes and algorithms. However, well-established data management systems, e.g., relational database management systems (RDBMSs) do not have query-specific algorithms and indexes. These systems build complex queries from simple building-block operators, e.g., SELECT, PROJECT, and GROUP BY. Also, these systems use query optimizers to build query evaluation pipelines that use efficient query plans to answer queries. Exiting SKDMSs neither have query optimizers nor building-block operators. The only proposal for spatial-keyword building-block operators is the Atlas [68] query language. Lee et al. [139] introduce a simple spatial-keyword optimizer that addresses only the spatial-keyword filter and top-k queries. This calls for the development of full-fledged spatial-keyword optimizers that can support complex spatial-keyword queries by arbitrating among the various query evaluation plans.

5.4   BIG SPATIO-TEMPORAL KEYWORD QUERY PROCESSING

Existing big SKDMSs focus on leveraging the spatial and textual properties of data and queries to optimize their processing. It is often the case that spatial-keyword data is associated with a temporal attribute. However, this temporal dimension is often neglected when dealing with spatial-keyword data. Integrating the time dimension in big SKDMSs requires new workload distribution and indexing techniques. There exist proposals for centralized spatio-temporal-keyword indexing, e.g., ST2I [53]. However, centralized systems are not scalable, and are restricted by the resources of the single machine they run on. This calls for the development of scalable spatio-temporal-keyword systems that use novel data distribution and indexing approaches.

Bibliography

[1] Facebook states. `http://newsroom.fb.com/company-info/` 2

[2] Twitter firehose. `http://developer.twitter.com/` 46

[3] OpenStreetMap. `www.openstreetmap.org` 59

[4] GNIP. `http://support.gnip.com/apis/powertrack/overview.html` 18, 70

[5] Trends map. `https://www.trendsmap.com` 5

[6] Pokemon Go. `www.pokemongo.com` 5, 6

[7] Internet live stats. `https://internetlivestats.com/` 2

[8] The TPC-H benchmark. `http://www.tpc.org/tpch/` 74

[9] The TripAdvisor website. `http://www.tripadvisor.com` 4

[10] Heatmap of Geotagged tweets talking about sunshine. `http://cartodb.s3.amazonaws.com/static_vizz/sunrise.html` 74

[11] The Waze application. `http://www.waze.com` 3, 4

[12] Google Maps. `http://www.maps.google.com` 3

[13] Apple Maps. `http://www.apple.com/ios/maps` 3

[14] Apache Spark. `http://spark.apache.org` 49, 50, 63, 70

[15] The AroundMe app. `http://www.aroundmeapp.com` 4

[16] D. Knuth. *The Art of Computer Programming*. Pearson Education, 1997. DOI: 10.1145/2491533.2491544 25, 26, 27, 34

[17] A. Dumey. Indexing for rapid random access memory systems. *Computers and Automation*, 5(12):6–9, 1956. 25

[18] H. Samet. *Foundations of Multidimensional and Metric Data Structures*. Morgan Kaufmann, 2006 28

[19] A. M. Aly, A. Sallam, B. M. Gnanasekaran, L.-V. Nguyen-Dinh, W. G. Aref, M. Ouzzani, and A. Ghafoor. M3: Stream processing on main-memory mapreduce. In *IEEE International Conference on Data Engineering (ICDE)*, pages 1253–1256, 2012. DOI: 10.1109/icde.2012.120 51

[20] D. Chamberlin, M. Astrahan, K. Eswaran, P. Griffiths, R. Lorie, J. Mehl, P. Reisner, and B. Wade. Sequel 2: A unified approach to data definition, manipulation, and control. *IBM Journal of Research and Development*, 20(6):560–575, 1976. DOI: 10.1147/rd.206.0560 7

[21] J. Nievergelt, H. Hinterberger, and K. Sevcik. The grid file: An adaptable, symmetric multikey file structure. *ACM Transactions on Database Systems (TODS)*, 9(1):38–71, 1984. 27
DOI: 10.1145/348.318586

[22] G. Hunter. Jackpine: A benchmark to evaluate spatial database performance. Ph.D. thesis, Department of Electrical Engineering and Computer Science, Princeton University, 1978. 28

[23] G. Hunter and K. Steiglitz. Operations on images using quad trees. In *IEEE Transactions on Pattern Analysis and Machine Intelligence*, pages 145–153, 1979. 28
DOI: 10.1109/tpami.1979.4766900

[24] S. Ray, B. Simion, and A. D. Brown. Jackpine: A benchmark to evaluate spatial database performance. In *IEEE International Conference on Data Engineering (ICDE)*, pages 1139–1150, 2011. DOI: 10.1109/icde.2011.5767929 74

[25] C. Düntgen, T. Behr, and R. H. Güting. Berlinmod: A benchmark for moving object databases. *The International Journal on Very Large Data Bases (VLDB)*, 18(6):1335–1368, 2009. DOI: 10.1007/s00778-009-0142-5 74

[26] L. Alarabi, A. Eldawy, R. Alghamdi, and M. F. Mokbel. TAREEG: A mapreduce-based web service for extracting spatial data from openstreetmap. In *ACM International Conference on Management of Data (SIGMOD)*, pages 897–900, 2014. DOI: 10.1145/2588555.2594528 59, 60

[27] A. M. Aly, A. R. Mahmood, M. S. Hassan, W. G. Aref, M. Ouzzani, H. Elmeleegy, and T. Qadah. AQWA: Adaptive query workload aware partitioning of big spatial data. *International Conference on Very Large Data Bases (VLDB)*, 8(13):2062–2073, 2015. DOI: 10.14778/2831360.2831361 73

[28] A. Eldawy and M. F. Mokbel SpatialHadoop: A mapreduce framework for spatial data. In *IEEE International Conference on Data Engineering (ICDE)*, pages 1352–1363, 2015. DOI: 10.1109/icde.2015.7113382 59

[29] A. Huang Similarity measures for text document clustering. In *The 6th New Zealand Computer Science Research Student Conference (NZCSRSC2008)*, pages 49–56, 2008. 10

[30] X. Cao, L. Chen, G. Cong, C. S. Jensen, Q. Qu, A. Skovsgaard, D. Wu, and M. L. Yiu. Spatial keyword querying. In *Conceptual Modeling*, pages 16–29. 2012. DOI: 10.1007/978-3-642-34002-4_2 7

[31] P. Dixon. Basics of oracle text retrieval. In *IEEE Data Engineering Bulletin*, pages 11–14, 2004. 18

[32] R. Hamilton and K. Nayak. Microsoft SQL Server full-text search. In *IEEE Data Engineering Bulletin*, pages 7–10, 2001. 18

[33] L. Chen, G. Cong, X. Cao, and K.-L. Tan. Temporal spatial-keyword top-k publish/-subscribe. In *IEEE International Conference on Data Engineering (ICDE)*, pages 255–266, 2015. DOI: 10.1109/icde.2015.7113289 9

[34] L. Chen, X. Lin, H. Hu, C. S. Jensen, and J. Xu. Answering why-not questions on spatial keyword top-k queries. In *IEEE International Conference on Data Engineering (ICDE)*, pages 279–290, 2015. DOI: 10.1109/icde.2015.7113291 9

[35] G. Cong and C. S. Jensen. Querying geo-textual data: Spatial keyword queries and beyond. In *ACM International Conference on Management of Data (SIGMOD)*, pages 2207–2212, 2016. DOI: 10.1145/2882903.2912572 7

[36] J. Dean and S. Ghemawat. MapReduce: Simplified data processing on large clusters. *Communications of the ACM*, 51(1):107–113, 2008. DOI: 10.1145/1327452.1327492 49, 50, 59, 70

[37] A. Bhattacharyya. On a measure of divergence between two multinomial populations. *Sankhyā: The Indian Journal of Statistics*, pages 401–406, 1946. 17

[38] W. G. Aref. Window-based query processing. In *Encyclopedia of Database Systems*, pages 3533–3538, Springer, 2009. DOI: 10.1007/978-1-4899-7993-3_468-2 15

[39] R. Motwani, J. Widom, A. Arasu, B. Babcock, S. Babu, M. Datar, G. S. Manku, C. Olston, J. Rosenstein, and R. Varma. Query processing, approximation, and resource management in a data stream management system. In *Biennial Conference on Innovative Data Systems Research (CIDR)*, pages 245–256, 2003. 15

[40] D. J. Abadi, D. Carney, U. Çetintemel, M. Cherniack, C. Convey, S. Lee, M. Stonebraker, N. Tatbul, and S. Zdonik. Aurora: A new model and architecture for data stream management. *The International Journal on Very Large Data Bases (VLDB)*, 12(2):120–139, 2003. DOI: 10.1007/s00778-003-0095-z 15

[41] B. Babcock, S. Babu, M. Datar, R. Motwani, and J. Widom. Models and issues in data stream systems. In *The 21st ACM SIGMOD-SIGACT-SIGART Symposium on Principles of Database Systems (PODS)*, pages 1–16, 2002. 15 DOI: 10.1145/543613.543615

[42] S. Chandrasekaran and M. J. Franklin. Streaming queries over streaming data. In *The International Conference on Very Large Data Bases (VLDB)*, pages 203–214, 2002. 15 DOI: 10.1016/b978-155860869-6/50026-3

[43] D. Knuth The art of computer programming. *Sorting and Searching*, Addison Wesley, 1973. 25, 32

[44] T.-D. Doudali. Performance evaluation of social networking services using a spatio-temporal and textual big data generator. National Technical University of Athens, Diploma Thesis, 2015. 75

[45] T. Ghanem, A. Elmagarmid, P. Larson, and W. Aref. Supporting views in data stream management systems. *ACM Transactions on Database Systems (TODS)*, 35(1):1, 2010. DOI: 10.1145/1670243.1670244 15

[46] T. Ghanem, W. Aref, and A. Elmagarmid. Exploiting predicate-window semantics over data streams. *ACM SIGMOD Record*, 35(1):3–8, 2006. DOI: 10.1145/1121995.1121996 15

[47] J. Fan, G. Li, L. Zhou, S. Chen, and J. Hu. Seal: Spatio-textual similarity search. *International Conference on Very Large Data Bases (VLDB)*, 5(9):824–835, 2012. DOI: 10.14778/2311906.2311910 8

[48] R. A. Finkel and J. L. Bentley. Quad trees a data structure for retrieval on composite keys. *Acta Informatica*, 4(1):1–9, 1974. DOI: 10.1007/bf00288933 17, 25, 28

[49] Y. Gao, Y. Wang, and S. Yi. Preference-aware top-k spatio-textual queries. In *International Conference on Web-Age Information Management (WAIM)*, pages 186–197, Springer, 2016. DOI: 10.1007/978-3-319-47121-1_16 9

[50] R. Göbel, A. Henrich, R. Niemann, and D. Blank. A hybrid index structure for geo-textual searches. In *The International Conference on Information and Knowledge Management (CIKM)*, pages 1625–1628, ACM, 2009. DOI: 10.1145/1645953.1646188 30

[51] Y. Hao, H. Cao, Y. Qi, C. Hu, S. Brahma, and J. Han. Efficient keyword search on graphs using mapreduce. In *IEEE International Conference on Big Data*, pages 2871–2873, 2015. DOI: 10.1109/bigdata.2015.7364106 53

[52] P. He, H. Xu, X. Zhao, and Z. Shen. Scalable collective spatial keyword query. In *International Conference on Data Engineering Workshops (ICDEW)*, pages 182–189, IEEE, 2015. DOI: 10.1109/icdew.2015.7129574 26, 63, 64

[53] T.-A. Hoang-Vu, H. T. Vo, and J. Freire. A unified index for spatio-temporal keyword queries. In *The International Conference on Information and Knowledge Management (CIKM)*, pages 135–144, ACM, 2016. DOI: 10.1145/2983323.2983751 31, 43, 75

[54] H. Hu, G. Li, Z. Bao, J. Feng, Y. Wu, Z. Gong, and Y. Xu. Top-k spatio-textual similarity join. *IEEE Transactions on Knowledge and Data Engineering (TKDE)*, 28(2):551–565, 2016. DOI: 10.1109/icde.2016.7498433 11

[55] J. Jiang, H. Lu, B. Yang, and B. Cui. Finding top-k local users in geo-tagged social media data. In *IEEE International Conference on Data Engineering (ICDE)*, pages 267–278, 2015. DOI: 10.1109/icde.2015.7113290 60, 61

[56] M. Jiang, A. W.-C. Fu, and R. C.-W. Wong. Exact top-k nearest keyword search in large networks. In *ACM International Conference on Management of Data (SIGMOD)*, pages 393–404, 2015. DOI: 10.1145/2723372.2749447 9

[57] S. Kulkarni, N. Bhagat, M. Fu, V. Kedigehalli, C. Kellogg, S. Mittal, J. M. Patel, K. Ramasamy, and S. Taneja. Twitter Heron: Stream processing at scale. In *ACM International Conference on Management of Data (SIGMOD)*, pages 239–250, 2015. DOI: 10.1145/2723372.2742788 50

[58] C.-A. Lai, J. Donahue, A. Musaev, and C. Pu. Nimbus: Tuning filters service on tweet streams. In *IEEE International Congress on Big Data*, pages 623–630, 2015. DOI: 10.1109/bigdatacongress.2015.95 2, 70, 71

[59] J. Li, H. Wang, J. Li, and H. Gao. Skyline for geo-textual data. *GeoInformatica*, 20(3):453–469, 2016. DOI: 10.1007/s10707-015-0243-9 31

[60] W. Li, W. Wang, and T. Jin. Evaluating spatial keyword queries under the mapreduce framework. In *International Conference on Database Systems for Advanced Applications (DASFAA)*, pages 251–261, Springer, 2012. DOI: 10.1007/978-3-642-29023-7_26 52

[61] S. Liu, G. Li, and J. Feng. Star-join: Spatio-textual similarity join. In *The International Conference on Information and Knowledge Management (CIKM)*, pages 2194–2198, ACM, 2012. DOI: 10.1145/2396761.2398600 11

[62] Z. Liu. Spatial approximate keyword query processing in cloud computing system. *International Journal of Database Theory and Application*, 8(2):81–94, 2015. DOI: 10.14257/ijdta.2015.8.2.09 17

[63] Y. Lu, M. Zhang, S. Witherspoon, Y. Yesha, Y. Yesha, and N. Rishe. Sksopen: Efficient indexing, querying, and visualization of geo-spatial big data. In *ICMLA*, vol. 2, pages 495–500, IEEE, 2013. DOI: 10.1109/icmla.2013.196 69, 70

[64] S. Luo, Y. Luo, S. Zhou, G. Cong, and J. Guan. Disks: A system for distributed spatial group keyword search on road networks. *International Conference on Very Large Data Bases (VLDB)*, 5(12):1966–1969, 2012. DOI: 10.14778/2367502.2367549 68, 69

[65] S. Luo, Y. Luo, S. Zhou, G. Cong, J. Guan, and Z. Yong. Distributed spatial keyword querying on road networks. In *International Conference on Extending Database Technology (EDBT)*, pages 235–246, Citeseer, 2014. 17, 68, 69

[66] Y. Ma, Y. Zhang, and X. Meng. St-hbase: A scalable data management system for massive geo-tagged objects. In *International Conference on Web-Age Information Management (WAIM)*, pages 155–166, Springer, 2013. 61, 62, 63, 64 DOI: 10.1007/978-3-642-38562-9_16

[67] A. Magdy, M. F. Mokbel, S. Elnikety, S. Nath, and Y. He. Venus: Scalable real-time spatial queries on microblogs with adaptive load shedding. *IEEE Transactions on Knowledge and Data Engineering (TKDE)*, 28(2):356–370, 2016. DOI: 10.1109/tkde.2015.2493531 28

[68] A. R. Mahmood, W. G. Aref, A. M. Aly, and M. Tang. Atlas: On the expression of spatial-keyword group queries using extended relational constructs. In *ACM SIGSPATIAL International Conference on Advances in Geographic Information Systems*, pages 45:1–45:10, 2016. DOI: 10.1145/2996913.2996987 18, 21, 22, 23, 75

[69] A. R. Mahmood and W. G. Aref. Query processing techniques for big spatial-keyword data. In *ACM International Conference on Management of Data (SIGMOD)*, pages 1777–1782, 2017. DOI: 10.1145/3035918.3054773 7

[70] K. Birman and T. Joseph. Exploiting virtual synchrony in distributed systems. *SIGOPS Operating Systems Review*, 21(5):123–138, November 1987. DOI: 10.21236/ada177091 55

[71] R. Mahmood, A. Daghistani, A. Aly, M. Tang, S. Basalamah, S. Prabhakar, and W. Aref. Adaptive spatial-keyword indexing over a distributed data streaming cluster. In *ACM SIGSPATIAL International Conference on Advances in Geographic Information Systems*, pages 219–228, 2018. 11, 31, 54, 65, 67, 73

[72] M. F. Mokbel, L. Alarabi, J. Bao, A. Eldawy, A. Magdy, M. Sarwat, E. Waytas, and S. Yackel. MNTG: An extensible web-based traffic generator. In *The International Symposium on Spatial and Temporal Databases (SSTD)*, pages 38–55, 2013. DOI: 10.1007/978-3-642-40235-7_3 74

[73] I. Mytilinis, I. Giannakopoulos, I. Konstantinou, K. Doka, D. Tsitsigkos, M. Ter-rovitis, L. Giampouras, and N. Koziris. Modissense: A distributed spatio-temporal and textual processing platform for social networking services. In *ACM International Conference on Management of Data (SIGMOD)*, pages 895–900, 2015. DOI: 10.1145/2723372.2735375 70

[74] J. B. Rocha-Junior, O. Gkorgkas, S. Jonassen, and K. Nørvåg. Efficient processing of top-k spatial keyword queries. In *International Symposium on Spatial and Temporal Databases*, pages 205–222, Springer, 2011. DOI: 10.1007/978-3-642-22922-0_13 17, 30, 39

[75] J. Sankaranarayanan, H. Samet, B. E. Teitler, M. D. Lieberman, and J. Sperling. Twit-terstand: News in tweets. In *ACM SIGSPATIAL International Conference on Advances in Geographic Information Systems*, pages 42–51, 2009. DOI: 10.1145/1653771.1653781 5, 46, 47

[76] K. Shvachko, H. Kuang, S. Radia, and R. Chansler. The hadoop distributed file system. In *MSST*, pages 1–10, IEEE, 2010. DOI: 10.1109/msst.2010.5496972 60, 61

[77] A. M. Aly, W. G Aref, and M. Ouzzani. Spatial queries with two KNN predicates. *International Conference on Very Large Data Bases (VLDB)*, 5(11):1100–1111, 2012. DOI: 10.14778/2350229.2350231 74

[78] B. E. Teitler, M. D. Lieberman, D. Panozzo, J. Sankaranarayanan, H. Samet, and J. Sperling. NewsStand: A new view on news. In *ACM SIGSPATIAL International Conference on Advances in Geographic Information Systems*, page 18:1–18:10, 2008. DOI: 10.1145/1463434.1463458 57, 58

[79] A. R. Mahmood, A. M. Aly, and W. G. Aref. FAST: Frequency-aware spatio-textual indexing for in-memory continuous filter query processing. In *IEEE International Conference on Data Engineering (ICDE)*, ACM, 2018. 15, 28, 34, 39, 41, 67

[80] B. Zheng, K. Zheng, X. Xiao, H. Su, H. Yin, Xi. Zhou, and G. Li. Keyword-aware continuous KNN query on road networks. In *IEEE International Conference on Data Engineering (ICDE)*, pages 871–882, 2016. DOI: 10.1109/icde.2016.7498297 15, 17

[81] Y. Fang, R. Cheng, G. Cong, N. Mamoulis, and Y. Li. On spatial pattern match-ing. In *IEEE International Conference on Data Engineering (ICDE)*, ACM, 2018. DOI: 10.1109/icde.2018.00035 14

[82] S. Vaid, C. B. Jones, H. Joho, and M. Sanderson. Spatio-textual indexing for geographical search on the Web. In *The International Symposium on Spatial and Temporal Databases (SSTD)*. pages 218–235, 2005. DOI: 10.1007/11535331_13 26, 32, 36, 38, 39

[83] S. Helmer and G. Moerkotte. A performance study of four index structures for set-valued attributes of low cardinality. *The International Journal on Very Large Data Bases (VLDB)*, 12(3):244–261, 2003. DOI: 10.1007/s00778-003-0106-0 32

[84] K. Kim, S. K. Cha, and K. Kwon. Optimizing multidimensional index trees for main memory access. In *ACM SIGMOD Record*, vol. 30, pages 139–150, 2001. DOI: 10.1145/376284.375679 30

[85] Z. Hmedeh, H. Kourdounakis, V. Christophides, C. Du Mouza, M. Scholl, and N. Travers. Subscription indexes for web syndication systems. In *The International Conference on Extending Database Technology (EDBT)*, pages 312–323, 2012. DOI: 10.1145/2247596.2247634 32, 33, 34

[86] C. Faloutsos and H. Jagadish. Hybrid index organizations for text databases. In *The International Conference on Extending Database Technology (EDBT)*, pages 310–327, 1992. DOI: 10.1007/bfb0032439 33, 36

[87] A. Toshniwal, S. Taneja, A. Shukla, K. Ramasamy, J. M. Patel, S. Kulkarni, J. Jackson, K. Gade, M. Fu, J. Donham, et al. Storm@ twitter. In *ACM International Conference on Management of Data (SIGMOD)*, pages 147–156, 2014. DOI: 10.1145/2588555.2595641 50, 54, 55, 56, 63, 65

[88] A. Magdy, A. Aly, M. Mokbel, S. Elnikety, Y. He, S. Nath, and W. Aref. GeoTrend: Spatial trending queries on real-time microblogs. *ACM SIGSPATIAL International Conference on Advances in Geographic Information Systems*, 2016. DOI: 10.1145/2996913.2996986 15, 28, 43, 44

[89] D. Sacharidis, P. Mehta, D. Skoutas, K. Patroumpas, and A. Voisard. Continuous summarization of streaming spatio-textual posts. In *ACM SIGSPATIAL International Conference on Advances in Geographic Information Systems*, pages 53:1–53:4, 2017. DOI: 10.1145/3139958.3140027 15

[90] P. Mehta. Spatial, temporal, and textual retrieval and analysis of geotagged posts. Ph.D. thesis, Freie Universität Berlin, 2018. 15

[91] B. Wang, R. Zhu, X. Yang, and G. Wang. Top-k representative documents query over geo-textual data stream. *World Wide Web*, 21(2):537–555, 2018. DOI: 10.1007/s11280-017-0470-0 15

[92] X. Wang, Y. Zhang, W. Zhang, X. Lin, and W. Wang. Selectivity estimation on streaming spatio-textual data using local correlations. *International Conference on Very Large Data Bases (VLDB)*, 8(2):101–112, 2014. DOI: 10.14778/2735471.2735472 15

[93] S. Oh, H. Jung, and U. Kim. An efficient processing of range spatial keyword queries over moving objects. In *Information Networking (ICOIN), International Conference on*, pages 525–530, IEEE, 2018. DOI: 10.1109/icoin.2018.8343174 15

[94] C. Salgado, M. Cheema, and M. Ali. Continuous monitoring of range spatial keyword query over moving objects. *International World Wide Web Conference (WWW)*, 21(3):687–712, 2018. DOI: 10.1007/s11280-017-0488-3 15

[95] X. Wang, W. Zhang, Y. Zhang, X. Lin, and Z. Huang. Top-k spatial-keyword publish/subscribe over sliding window. *The International Journal on Very Large Data Bases (VLDBJ)*, pages 1–26, 2016. DOI: 10.14778/2904483.2904490 17, 55, 56, 63

[96] X. Wang, Y. Zhang, W. Zhang, X. Lin, and Z. Huang. Skype: Top-k spatial-keyword publish/subscribe over sliding window. *International Conference on Very Large Data Bases (VLDB)*, 9(7):588–599, 2016. DOI: 10.14778/2904483.2904490 15, 45, 46

[97] A. Skovsgaard, D. Sidlauskas, and C. Jensen. Scalable top-k spatio-temporal term querying. *IEEE International Conference on Data Engineering (ICDE)*, pages 148–159, 2014. DOI: 10.1109/icde.2014.6816647 17, 45

[98] D. Comer. Ubiquitous B-tree. *ACM Computing Surveys (CSUR)*, 11(2):121–137, 1979. DOI: 10.1145/356770.356776 25, 30

[99] X. Wang, Y. Zhang, W. Zhang, X. Lin, and W. Wang. AP-tree: Efficiently support continuous spatial-keyword queries over stream. In *IEEE International Conference on Data Engineering (ICDE)*, pages 1107–1118, 2015. DOI: 10.1109/icde.2015.7113360 15, 28, 34, 40

[100] H. Wiki. Hbase: Bigtable-like structured storage for hadoop HDFS. http://wiki.a pache.org/hadoop/Hbase, 2012. 61, 70

[101] D. Wu and C. S. Jensen. A density-based approach to the retrieval of top-k spatial textual clusters. In *The International Conference on Information and Knowledge Management (CIKM)*, pages 2095–2100, ACM, 2016. DOI: 10.1145/2983323.2983648 12

[102] D. Wu, M. L. Yiu, G. Cong, and C. S. Jensen. Joint top-k spatial keyword query processing. *IEEE Transactions on Knowledge and Data Engineering (TKDE)*, 24(10):1889–1903, 2012. DOI: 10.1109/tkde.2011.172 9

[103] J. Yang, W. Zhang, Y. Zhang, X. Wang, and X. Lin. Categorical top-k spatial influence query. *International World Wide Web Conference (WWW)*, pages 1–29, 2016. DOI: 10.1007/s11280-016-0383-3 9

[104] M. Yang, L. Zheng, Y. Lu, M. Guo, and J. Li. Cloud-assisted spatio-textual k nearest neighbor joins in sensor networks. In *INISCom*, pages 12–17, IEEE, 2015. DOI: 10.4108/icst.iniscom.2015.258321 54

[105] M. Zaharia, M. Chowdhury, T. Das, A. Dave, J. Ma, M. McCauley, M. J. Franklin, S. Shenker, and I. Stoica. Resilient distributed datasets: A fault-tolerant abstraction for in-memory cluster computing. In *USENIX conference on Networked Systems Design and Implementation*, page 2, USENIX Association, 2012. 50

[106] M. Zaharia, T. Das, H. Li, T. Hunter, S. Shenker, and I. Stoica. Discretized streams: Fault-tolerant streaming computation at scale. In *ACM Symposium on Operating Systems Principles (SOSP)*, pages 423–438, 2013. DOI: 10.1145/2517349.2522737 51, 70

[107] C. Zhang, Y. Zhang, W. Zhang, and X. Lin. Inverted linear quadtree: Efficient top-k spatial keyword search. *IEEE Transactions on Knowledge and Data Engineering (TKDE)*, 28(7):1706–1721, 2016. DOI: 10.1109/icde.2013.6544884 28

[108] M. Zhang, H. Wang, Y. Lu, T. Li, Y. Guang, C. Liu, E. Edrosa, H. Li, and N. Rishe. Terrafly geocloud: An online spatial data analysis and visualization system. *ACM Transactions on Intelligent Systems and Technology (TIST)*, 6(3):34, 2015. DOI: 10.1145/2505515.2508206 69, 70

[109] Y. Zhang, Y. Ma, and X. Meng. Efficient spatio-textual similarity join using mapreduce. In *Web Intelligence (WI) and Intelligent Agent Technologies (IAT)*, vol. 1, pages 52–59, 2014. DOI: 10.1109/wi-iat.2014.16 11

[110] Y. Zhang, Y.-Z. Ma, and X.-F. Meng. Efficient processing of spatial keyword queries on HBase. *Journal of Chinese Computer Systems*, 33(10):2141–2146, 2012. 31

[111] K. Zheng, B. Zheng, J. Xu, G. Liu, A. Liu, and Z. Li. Popularity-aware spatial keyword search on activity trajectories. *International World Wide Web Conference (WWW)*, pages 1–25, 2016. DOI: 10.1007/s11280-016-0414-0 32

[112] J. Zobel and A. Moffat. Inverted files for text search engines. *ACM Computing Surveys (CSUR)*, 38(2):6, 2006. DOI: 10.1145/1132956.1132959 32

[113] A. Aitchison. *Beginning Spatial with SQL Server 2008*. Apress, 2009. DOI: 10.1007/978-1-4302-1830-2 17

[114] S. Alsubaiee, A. Behm, and C. Li. Supporting location-based approximate-keyword queries. In *ACM SIGSPATIAL International Conference on Advances in Geographic Information Systems*, pages 61–70, 2010. DOI: 10.1145/1869790.1869802 17

[115] W. G. Aref and H. Samet. Extending a DBMS with spatial operations. In *Symposium in Spatial Databases*, pages 297–318, 1991. DOI: 10.1007/3-540-54414-3_44 17

[116] N. Beckmann, H.-P. Kriegel, R. Schneider, and B. Seeger. The R*-tree: An efficient and robust access method for points and rectangles, *ACM International Conference on Management of Data (SIGMOD)*, vol. 19, pages 322–331, 1990. DOI: 10.1145/93597.98741 25, 30, 37

[117] P. Zhang, H. Lin, B. Yao, and D. Lu. Level-aware collective spatial keyword queries. *Information Sciences*, 378:194–214, 2017. DOI: 10.1016/j.ins.2016.10.033 14, 17

[118] D. Choi, J. Pei, and X. Lin. Finding the minimum spatial keyword cover. In *IEEE International Conference on Data Engineering (ICDE)*, pages 685–696, 2016. DOI: 10.1109/icde.2016.7498281 12

[119] H. Chan, C. Long, and R. Wong. On generalizing collective spatial keyword queries. *IEEE Transactions on Knowledge and Data Engineering (TKDE)*, 30(9):1712–1726, 2018. DOI: 10.1109/tkde.2018.2800746 12, 17

[120] S. Su, S.Zhao, X. Cheng, R. Bi, X. Cao, and J. Wang. Group-based collective keyword querying in road networks. *Information Processing Letters*, 118:83–90, 2017. DOI: 10.1016/j.ipl.2016.10.008 13, 17

[121] P. Bouros, S. Ge, and N. Mamoulis. Spatio-textual similarity joins. *International Conference on Very Large Data Bases (VLDB)*, 6(1):1–12, 2012. DOI: 10.14778/2428536.2428537 11

[122] X. Cao, G. Cong, T. Guo, C. S. Jensen, and B. C. Ooi. Efficient processing of spatial group keyword queries. *ACM Transactions on Database Systems (TODS)*, 40(2):13, 2015. DOI: 10.1145/2772600 12, 13

[123] X. Cao, G. Cong, C. S. Jensen, and B. C. Ooi. Collective spatial keyword querying. In *ACM International Conference on Management of Data (SIGMOD)*, pages 373–384, 2011. DOI: 10.1145/1989323.1989363 12, 13

[124] A. Cary, O. Wolfson, and N. Rishe. Efficient and scalable method for processing top-k spatial Boolean queries. In *Scientific and Statistical Database Management Conference (SSDBM)*, pages 87–95, 2010. DOI: 10.1007/978-3-642-13818-8_8 9, 10

[125] L. Chen, G. Cong, C. S. Jensen, and D. Wu. Spatial keyword query processing: An experimental evaluation. In *International Conference on Very Large Data Bases (VLDB)*, vol. 6, pages 217–228, 2013. DOI: 10.14778/2535569.2448955 25, 35, 38, 75

[126] M. Christoforaki, J. He, C. Dimopoulos, A. Markowetz, and T. Suel. Text vs. space: Efficient geo-search query processing. In *The International Conference on Information and Knowledge Management (CIKM)*, pages 423–432, 2011. DOI: 10.1145/2063576.2063641 30

[127] G. Cong, C. S. Jensen, and D. Wu. Efficient retrieval of the top-k most relevant spatial web objects. *International Conference on Very Large Data Bases (VLDB)*, 2(1):337–348, 2009. DOI: 10.14778/1687627.1687666 11

[128] C. Corley and R. Mihalcea. Measuring the semantic similarity of texts. In *ACL Workshop on Empirical Modeling of Semantic Equivalence and Entailment*, pages 13–18, 2005. DOI: 10.3115/1631862.1631865 10

[129] I. De Felipe, V. Hristidis, and N. Rishe. Keyword search on spatial databases. In *IEEE International Conference on Data Engineering (ICDE)*, pages 656–665, 2008. DOI: 10.1109/icde.2008.4497474 30, 34, 37

[130] M. J. Egenhofer. Spatial SQL: A query and presentation language. *IEEE Transactions on Knowledge and Data Engineering (TKDE)*, 6(1):86–95, 1994. DOI: 10.1109/69.273029 17

[131] S. G. Greener and S. Ravada. *Applying and Extending Oracle Spatial*, Packt Publishing Ltd., 2013. 17

[132] T. Guo, X. Cao, and G. Cong. Efficient algorithms for answering the m-closest keywords query. In *ACM International Conference on Management of Data (SIGMOD)*, pages 405–418, 2015. DOI: 10.1145/2723372.2723723 12

[133] A. Guttman. R-trees: A dynamic index structure for spatial searching, In *ACM International Conference on Management of Data (SIGMOD)*, pages 47–57, 1984. DOI: 10.1145/602264.602266 25, 30

[134] R. Hariharan, B. Hore, C. Li, and S. Mehrotra. Processing spatial-keyword (SK) queries in geographic information retrieval (GIR) systems. In *Scientific and Statistical Database Management Conference (SSBDM)*, page 16, 2007. DOI: 10.1109/ssdbm.2007.22 32

[135] W. Huang, G. Li, K.-L. Tan, and J. Feng. Efficient safe-region construction for moving top-k spatial keyword queries. In *International Conference on Information and Knowledge Management (CIKM)*, pages 932–941, 2012. DOI: 10.1145/2396761.2396879 9

[136] A. Khodaei, C. Shahabi, and C. Li. Hybrid indexing and seamless ranking of spatial and textual features of web documents. In *Database and Expert Systems Applications Conference (DEXA)*, pages 450–466, 2010. DOI: 10.1007/978-3-642-15364-8_37 32

[137] L. Neumeyer, B. Robbins, A. Nair, and A. Kesari. S4: Distributed stream computing platform. In *International Conference on Data Mining Workshops (ICDMW)*, pages 170–177, 2010. DOI: 10.1109/icdmw.2010.172 50

[138] S. George and A. Lee. *Linear Regression Analysis*. John Wiley & Sons, 2012. DOI: 10.1002/9780471722199 50

[139] T. Lee, J.-W. Park, S. Lee, S.-W. Hwang, S. Elnikety, and Y. He. Processing and op-timizing main memory spatial-keyword queries. *International Conference on Very Large Data Bases (VLDB)*, 9(3):132–143, 2015. DOI: 10.14778/2850583.2850588 42, 75

[140] S. Tanimoto and T. Pavlidis. A hierarchical data structure for picture processing. *Computer Graphics and Image Processing*, 4(2):104–119, 1975. DOI: 10.1016/s0146-664x(75)80003-7 28, 36

[141] W. Aref and H. Samet. Efficient processing of window queries in the pyramid data structure.. *ACM SIGACT-SIGMOD-SIGART Symposium on Principles of Database Systems (PODS)*, pages 265–272, 1990. DOI: 10.1145/298514.298579 25, 28, 36, 41

[142] G. Li, J. Feng, and J. Xu. Desks: Direction-aware spatial keyword search. In *IEEE International Conference on Data Engineering (ICDE)*, pages 474–485, 2012. DOI: 10.1109/icde.2012.93 10

[143] Z. Li, K. C. Lee, B. Zheng, W.-C. Lee, D. Lee, and X. Wang. IR-tree: An efficient index for geographic document search. *IEEE Transactions on Knowledge and Data Engineering (TKDE)*, 23(4):585–599, 2011. DOI: 10.1109/tkde.2010.149 9, 30, 32, 37, 46

[144] J. Lu, Y. Lu, and G. Cong. Reverse spatial and textual k nearest neighbor search. In *ACM International Conference on Management of Data (SIGMOD)*, pages 349–360, 2011. DOI: 10.1145/1989323.1989361 11

[145] Y. Lu, J. Lu, G. Cong, W. Wu, and C. Shahabi. Efficient algorithms and cost models for reverse spatial-keyword k-nearest neighbor search. *ACM Transactions on Database Systems (TODS)*, 39(2):13, 2014. DOI: 10.1145/2576232 11

[146] A. Magdy, L. Alarabi, S. Al-Harthi, M. Musleh, T. M. Ghanem, S. Ghani, and M. F. Mokbel. Taghreed: A system for querying, analyzing, and visualizing geotagged microblogs. In *ACM SIGSPATIAL International Conference on Advances in Geographic Information Systems*, pages 163–172, 2014. DOI: 10.1109/icde.2015.7113390 16, 28, 57, 58, 65, 66

[147] T. Bray. The javascript object notation (JSON) data interchange format. RFC Ed., 2017. DOI: 10.17487/rfc7159 18

[148] R. Bayer and E. McCreight. Organization and maintenance of large ordered indices. In *Proc. of the ACM SIGFIDET (now SIGMOD) Workshop on Data Description, Access and Control*, pages 107–141, 1970. DOI: 10.21236/ad0712079 25

[149] P. Zhang, H. Lin, Y. Gao, and D. Lu. Aggregate keyword nearest neighbor queries on road networks. *GeoInformatica Journal*, 22(2):237–268, 2018. DOI: 10.1007/s10707-017-0315-0 16, 17

[150] A. Magdy and M. F. Mokbel. Towards a microblogs data management system. In *International Conference on Mobile Data Management (MDM)*, pages 271–278, 2015. DOI: 10.1109/mdm.2015.24 18, 20

[151] D. Wu, Y. Li, B. Choi, and J. Xu. Social-aware top-k spatial keyword search. In *International Conference on Mobile Data Management (MDM)*, pages 235–244, 2014. DOI: 10.1109/mdm.2014.35 9, 10

[152] A. R. Mahmood, A. M. Aly, T. Qadah, E. K. Rezig, A. Daghistani, A. Madkour, A. S. Abdelhamid, M. S. Hassan, W. G. Aref, and S. Basalamah. Tornado: A distributed spatio-textual stream processing system. *International Conference on Very Large Data Bases (VLDB)*, 8(12):2020–2023, 2015. DOI: 10.14778/2824032.2824126 11, 54, 65, 67, 73

[153] Z. Chen, G. Cong, Z. Zhang, T. Z. Fuz, and L. Chen Distributed publish/subscribe query processing on the spatio-textual data stream. In *IEEE International Conference on Data Engineering (ICDE)*, pages 1095–1106, 2017. DOI: 10.1109/icde.2017.154 56, 57, 68, 73

[154] J. Martinez-Gil. An overview of textual semantic similarity measures based on web intelligence. *Artificial Intelligence Review*, 42(4):935–943, 2014. DOI: 10.31219/osf.io/ka26r 10

[155] J. Melton and A. Eisenberg. SQL multimedia and application packages (SQL/mm). *ACM Sigmod Record*, 30(4):97–102, 2001. DOI: 10.1145/604264.604280 17

[156] M. Tang, R. Y. Tahboub, W. G. Aref, M. J. Atallah, Q. M. Malluhi, M. Ouzzani, and Y. N. Silva. Similarity group-by operators for multi-dimensional relational data. *IEEE Transactions on Knowledge and Data Engineering (TKDE)*, 28(2):510–523, 2016. DOI: 10.1109/icde.2016.7498368 22

[157] B. C. Ooi, K. J. McDonell, and R. Sacks-Davis. Spatial KD-tree: An indexing mechanism for spatial databases. In *IEEE Computer Society Signature Conference on Computers, Software and Applications (IEEE COMPSAC)*, pages 433–438, 1987. 31

[158] J. L. Bentley. Multidimensional binary search trees used for associative searching. *Communications of the ACM*, 18(9):509–517, 1975. DOI: 10.1145/361002.361007 31, 43, 62, 68

[159] C. Faloutsos and S. Christodoulakis. Signature files: An access method for documents and its analytical performance evaluation. *ACM Transactions on Information Systems (TOIS)*, 2(4):267–288, 1984. DOI: 10.1145/2275.357411 33, 37

[160] R. De La Briandais. File searching using variable length keys. In *Western Joint Computer Conference*, pages 295–298, March 3–5, 1959. DOI: 10.1145/1457838.1457895 34

[161] J. Park and S.-G. Lee. Keyword search in relational databases. *Knowledge and Information Systems*, 26(2):175–193, 2011. DOI: 10.1007/s10115-010-0284-1 17

[162] P. Rigaux, M. Scholl, and A. Voisard. *Spatial Databases: with Application to GIS*. Morgan Kaufmann, 2001. 17

[163] J. B. Rocha-Junior and K. Nørvåg. Top-k spatial keyword queries on road networks. In *International Conference on Extending Database Technology (EDBT)*, pages 168–179, 2012. DOI: 10.1145/2247596.2247617 17

[164] H. Samet. *The Design and Analysis of Spatial Data Structures*, vol. 85, Addison-Wesley, Reading, MA, 1990.

[165] A. Skovsgaard and C. S. Jensen. Finding top-k relevant groups of spatial web objects. *The International Journal on Very Large Data Bases (VLDB)*, 24(4):537–555, 2015. DOI: 10.1007/s00778-015-0388-z 12, 14

[166] K. Stockinger, J. Cieslewicz, K. Wu, D. Rotem, and A. Shoshani. Using bitmap index for joint queries on structured and text data. In *New Trends in Data Warehousing and Data Analysis*, pages 1–23, 2009. DOI: 10.1007/978-0-387-87431-9_9 33

[167] A. Tomasic, H. Garcia-Molina, and K. Shoens. Incremental updates of inverted lists for text document retrieval *ACM SIGMOD Record*, 23(2):289–300, 1994. DOI: 10.1145/191843.191896 32

[168] S. Wang and K.-L. Zhang. Searching databases with keywords. *Journal of Computer Science and Technology*, 20(1):55–62, 2005. DOI: 10.1007/s11390-005-0006-4 17

[169] D. Wu, M. L. Yiu, C. S. Jensen, and G. Cong. Efficient continuously moving top-k spatial keyword query processing. In *IEEE International Conference on Data Engineering (ICDE)*, pages 541–552, 2011. DOI: 10.1109/icde.2011.5767861 15

[170] A. Arasu, S. Chaudhuri, K. Ganjam, and R. Kaushik. Incorporating string transformations in record matching. In *ACM International Conference on Management of Data (SIGMOD)*, pages 1231–1234, 2008. DOI: 10.1145/1376616.1376742 17

[171] P. Ahmed, M. Hasan, A. Kashyap, V. Hristidis, and V. J. Tsotras Efficient computation of top-k frequent terms over spatio-temporal ranges. In *ACM International Conference on Management of Data (SIGMOD)*, pages 1227–1241, 2017. DOI: 10.1145/3035918.3064032 16

[172] D. Zhang, B. Ooi, and A. Tung. Locating mapped resources in Web 2.0. In *IEEE International Conference on Data Engineering (ICDE)*, pages 521–532, 2010. DOI: 10.1109/icde.2010.5447897 12

[173] B. Yao, F. Li, M. Hadjieleftheriou, and K. Hou. Approximate string search in spatial databases. In *IEEE International Conference on Data Engineering (ICDE)*, pages 545–556, 2010. DOI: 10.1109/icde.2010.5447836 17

[174] D. Zhang, Y. M. Chee, A. Mondal, A. K. Tung, and M. Kitsuregawa. Keyword search in spatial databases: Towards searching by document. In *IEEE International Conference on Data Engineering (ICDE)*, pages 688–699, 2009. DOI: 10.1109/icde.2009.77 12, 33, 37, 38

[175] R. Kothuri, E. Beinat, and A. Godfrind. *Pro Oracle Spatial*. Apress, 2004. DOI: 10.1007/978-1-4302-0735-1 17

[176] N. Gramsky and H. Samet. Seeder finder: Identifying additional needles in the Twitter haystack. In *Proc. of the 6th ACM SIGSPATIAL International Workshop on Location-Based Social Networks*, pages 44–53, 2013. DOI: 10.1145/2536689.2536808 46

[177] A. Jackoway, H. Samet, and S. Jagan. Identification of live news events using Twitter. In *Proc. of the 3rd ACM SIGSPATIAL International Workshop on Location-Based Social Networks*, pages 25–32, 2011. DOI: 10.1145/2063212.2063224 5

[178] H. Wei, J. Sankaranarayanan, and H. Samet. Finding and tracking local Twitter users for news detection. In *ACM SIGSPATIAL International Conference on Advances in Geographic Information Systems*, pages 64:1–64:4, 2017. DOI: 10.1145/3139958.3141797 5, 46

[179] H. Wei, J. Sankaranarayanan, and H. Samet. Measuring spatial influence of Twitter users by interactions. In *Proc. of the 1st ACM SIGSPATIAL Workshop on Analytics for Local Events and News*, pages 2.1–2.10, 2017. DOI: 10.1145/3148044.3148046 5

[180] F. Wajid, H. Wei, and H. Samet. Identifying short-names for place entities from social networks. In *Proc. of the 1st ACM SIGSPATIAL Workshop on Recommendations for Location-based Services and Social Networks*, pages 4.1–4.4, 2017. DOI: 10.1145/3148150.3148157 5

[181] M. Lieberman and H. Samet. Multifaceted toponym recognition for streaming news. In *Proc. of the 34th International ACM SIGIR Conference on Research and Development in Information Retrieval*, pages 843–852, 2011. DOI: 10.1145/2009916.2010029 57

[182] K. Zheng, H. Su, B. Zheng, S. Shang, J. Xu, J. Liu, and X. Zhou. Interactive top-k spatial keyword queries. In *IEEE International Conference on Data Engineering (ICDE)*, pages 423–434, 2015. DOI: 10.1109/icde.2015.7113303 9

[183] M. Lieberman and H. Samet. Adaptive context features for toponym resolution in streaming news. In *Proc. of the 35th International ACM SIGIR Conference on Research and Development in Information Retrieval*, pages 731–740, 2012. DOI: 10.1145/2348283.2348381 46, 57

[184] M. Lieberman and H. Samet.   Supporting rapid processing and interactive map-based exploration of streaming news. In *ACM SIGSPATIAL International Conference on Advances in Geographic Information Systems (SIGSPATIAL)*, pages 179–188, 2012. DOI: 10.1145/2424321.2424345

[185] M. Lieberman, H. Samet, and J. Sankaranarayanan. Geotagging: Using proximity, sibling, and prominence clues to understand comma groups. In *Proc. of the 6th Workshop on Geographic Information Retrieval*, pages 6.1–6.8, 2010. DOI: 10.1145/1722080.1722088

[186] M. Lieberman, H. Samet, and J. Sankaranarayanan.   Geotagging with local lexicons to build indexes for textually-specified spatial data. In *IEEE International Conference on Data Engineering (ICDE)*, pages 201–212, 2010. DOI: 10.1109/icde.2010.5447903

[187] J. Sankaranarayanan and H. Samet.   Images in news. In *International Conference on Pattern Recognition (ICPR)*, pages 3240–3243, 2010. DOI: 10.1109/icpr.2010.792

[188] H. Samet, B. Teitler, M. Adelfio, and M. Lieberman. Adapting a map query interface for a gesturing touch screen interface. In *International World Wide Web Conference (WWW)*, pages 257–260, 2011. DOI: 10.1145/1963192.1963303

[189] G. Quercini, H. Samet, J. Sankaranarayanan, and M. Lieberman. Determining the spatial reader scopes of news sources using local lexicons. In *ACM SIGSPATIAL International Conference on Advances in Geographic Information Systems (SIGSPATIAL)*, pages 43–52, 2010. DOI: 10.1145/1869790.1869800

[190] H. Samet, M. Adelfio, B. Fruin, M. Lieberman, and B. Teitler.   Porting a web-based mapping application to a smartphone app. In *ACM SIGSPATIAL International Conference on Advances in Geographic Information Systems (SIGSPATIAL)*, pages 525–528, 2011. DOI: 10.1145/2093973.2094065

[191] H. Samet, J. Sankaranarayanan, M. Lieberman, M. Adelfio, B. Fruin, J. Lotkowski, D. Panozzo, J. Sperling, and B. Teitler. Reading news with maps by exploiting spatial synonyms. In *Communications of the ACM*, pages 564–77, 2014. DOI: 10.1145/2629572

[192] A. Abdelkader, E. Hand, and H. Samet.   Brands in NewsStand: Spatio-temporal browsing of business news.   In *ACM SIGSPATIAL International Conference on Advances in Geographic Information Systems (SIGSPATIAL)*, pages 97:1–97:4, 2015. DOI: 10.1145/2820783.2820795 57

[193] M. Lieberman, H. Samet, J. Sankaranarayanan, and J. Sperling. STEWARD: Architecture of a spatio-textual search engine. In *ACM SIGSPATIAL International Conference on Advances in Geographic Information Systems (SIGSPATIAL)*, pages 25:1–25:8, 2007. DOI: 10.1145/1341012.1341045 3

[194] M. Lieberman, H. Samet, J. Sankaranarayanan, and J. Sperling. Spatio-textual spread-sheets: Geotagging via spatial coherence. In *ACM SIGSPATIAL International Conference on Advances in Geographic Information Systems (SIGSPATIAL)*, pages 524–527, 2009. DOI: 10.1145/1653771.1653860

[195] G. Quercini and H. Samet. Uncovering the spatial relatedness in Wikipedia. In *ACM SIGSPATIAL International Conference on Advances in Geographic Information Systems (SIGSPATIAL)*, pages 153–162, 2014. DOI: 10.1145/2666310.2666398 3

[196] C. Fu, J. Sankaranarayanan, and H. Samet. WeiboStand: Capturing Chinese breaking news using Weibo tweets. In *ACM SIGSPATIAL International Conference on Advances in Geographic Information Systems (SIGSPATIAL)*, pages 41–48, 2014. DOI: 10.1145/2755492.2755499 5

[197] G. Hjaltason and H. Samet. Speeding up construction of PMR quadtree-based spatial indexes. In *The International Journal on Very Large Data Bases (VLDB)*, pages 109–137, 2002. DOI: 10.1007/s00778-002-0067-8 28

[198] H. Samet. Sorting in space and words. In *IEEE International Conference on Data Engineering (ICDE)*, 2018. DOI: 10.1109/icde.2018.00222 25

[199] M. Adelfio and H. Samet. Geowhiz: Using common categories for toponym resolution. In *ACM SIGSPATIAL International Conference on Advances in Geographic Information Systems (SIGSPATIAL)*, pages 542–545, 2013. 5

[200] R. Lan, M. Adelfio, and H. Samet. Spatio-temporal disease tracking using news articles. In *Proc. of the 3rd ACM SIGSPATIAL International Workshop on the use of GIS in Public Health*, pages 31–38, 2014. DOI: 10.1145/2676629.2676637 5

[201] R. Lan, M. Lieberman, and H. Samet. The picture of health: Map-based, collaborative spatio-temporal disease tracking. In *Proc. of the 1st ACM SIGSPATIAL International Workshop on use of GIS in Public Health*, pages 27–35, 2012. DOI: 10.1145/2452516.2452522 5

[202] H. Samet. A quadtree medial axis transform. *Communications of the ACM*, 26(9):680–693, 1983. DOI: 10.21236/ada086097 28

[203] H. Samet. A top-down quadtree traversal algorithm. *IEEE Transactions on Pattern Analysis and Machine Intelligence*, (1):94–98, 1985. DOI: 10.1109/tpami.1985.4767622

[204] H. Samet and R. Webber. On encoding boundaries with quadtrees. *IEEE Transactions on Pattern Analysis and Machine Intelligence*, (3):365–369, 1984. DOI: 10.1109/t-pami.1984.4767529

[205] R. Sivan and H. Samet. Algorithms for constructing quadtree surface maps. In *Proc. 5th International Symposium on Spatial Data Handling*, pages 361–370, 1992.

[206] E. Tanin, A. Harwood, and H. Samet. A distributed quadtree index for peer-to-peer settings. In *IEEE International Conference on Data Engineering (ICDE)*, pages 254–255, 2005. DOI: 10.1109/icde.2005.7 28

[207] L. Chen, G. Cong, and X. Cao. An efficient query indexing mechanism for filtering geo-textual data. In *ACM International Conference on Management of Data (SIGMOD)*, pages 749–760, 2013. DOI: 10.1145/2463676.2465328 15

[208] G. Li, Y. Wang, T. Wang, and J. Feng. Location-aware publish/subscribe. In *ACM International Conference on Knowledge Discovery and Data Mining (SIGKDD)*, pages 802–810, 2013. DOI: 10.1145/2487575.2487617 15

[209] P. Ramsey. PostGIS manual. In *Refractions Research Inc.*, 2005. 17

[210] A. Piórkowski. MySQL spatial and PostCIS implementations of spatial data standards. In *EJPAU*, 14(1):3, 2011. 17

Authors' Biographies

AHMED R. MAHMOOD

Ahmed R. Mahmood is a Ph.D. candidate at the Department of Computer Science, Purdue University. His research interests are big data, database systems, spatial, spatial-keyword, and distributed stream processing. He is the first-place winner of the 2017 ACM SIGSPATIAL student research competition. He has been awarded the Purdue CS Teaching Fellowship, the Teaching Academy Graduate Teaching Award, and the Raymond Boyce Graduate Teacher Award. Ahmed is the main designer and developer of Tornado, the first distributed spatial-keyword stream processing system. He published several scholarly articles in the area of spatial and spatial-keyword processing in top venues including ACM SIGSPATIAL, ICDE, and VLDB. For more information, please visit: http://www.cs.purdue.edu/homes/amahmoo.

WALID G. AREF

Walid G. Aref is a professor of Computer Science at Purdue. His research interests are in the areas of database systems, spatial and spatio-temporal data systems, data streaming, indexing, and query processing techniques. His research has been supported by the NSF, the National Institute of Health, Purdue Research Foundation, Qatar National Research Foundation, CERIAS, Panasonic, and Microsoft Corp. In 2001, he received the CAREER Award from the National Science Foundation and in 2004, he received a Purdue University Faculty Scholar award. Walid is an IEEE Fellow. He has received several best-paper awards including the 2016 VLDB 10-Year Best-Paper award. Walid is the Editor-in-Chief of the *ACM Transactions of Spatial Algorithms and Systems (TSAS)*, and has been an associate editor of the *ACM Transactions of Database Systems (TODS)*, an editor of the *VLDB Journal*, and an editor of the *Journal of Spatial Information Science (JOSIS)*. He has been one of the co-founders and a past chair of the ACM SIGSPATIAL Special Interest Group. For more information, please visit: http://www.cs.purdue.edu/homes/aref.